THE HIGH FORTRESS

A Guide to the Rock of Dunamase

Edited by Peigín Doyle

Word*well*

THE HIGH FORTRESS:
A Guide to the Rock of Dunamase

First published 2022
by Wordwell Ltd,
in association with Laois County Council.

Wordwell Ltd.,
Unit 9, 78 Furze Road,
Sandyford Industrial Estate,
Dublin 18, Eircode D18 C6V6
T: +353-1-2933568
www.wordwellbooks.com
ISBN 978-1-913934-74-3

Acknowledgements:
This publication has been funded by The Heritage Council and Laois County Council. An action of the Laois Heritage and Biodiversity Strategy 2021–2025.

Contributors:
Dr John Feehan
Dr Sharon Greene
Dr Matthew Stout
Brian Hodkinson
Editor: Peigín Doyle
Commissioning editor: Catherine Casey
Series commissioning editor: Una MacConville
Production editor: Nick Maxwell
Design: Ger Garland
Layout: © Wordwell Ltd.
Printer: W & G Bairds, Antrim.

An Chomhairle Oidhreachta
The Heritage Council

Laois County Council
Áras an Chontae, Portlaoise, Co. Laois

CONTENTS

Dunamase as it looked in 1794, recorded in *Grosse's Antiquities*.

FOREWORD

As *Cathaoirleach* of Laois County Council I am proud to introduce this wonderful book on the Rock of Dunamase. The lavishly-illustrated guide is a must-read for anyone exploring this fortified crag or learning about the history of Laois. The book is the result of a collaborative process between the Laois Heritage Forum and the authors, under the expert guidance of Wordwell Books. I would like to thank all involved and congratulate all the contributing authors and the editor on a truly groundbreaking publication. The continued involvement of The Heritage Council in supporting and developing all aspects of the heritage of Laois must be especially acknowledged.

The ruins of an Anglo-Norman fortress built over an Early Christian Irish *dún*, Dunamase was fought over, occupied, fortified, reinforced, seized, abandoned and blown up. Today, silhouetted against the Laois skyline, the stark grandeur of the ruined fortress of Dunamase has the power still to stir our imaginations.

Plundered by Viking raiders in AD 843, it became part of the dowry of Aoife, the bartered daughter of Diarmait Mac Murchada. She married Richard de Clare, commonly known as Strongbow, as the price for the Anglo-Norman invaders restoring Diarmait as king of Leinster.

Fortified by a murder hole, arrow slits, portcullis, drawbridge and high protecting walls, the struggles between Gaelic Irish versus invading forces played out around the fortress of Dunamase for centuries. The discovery by archaeologists of 10 beheaded skulls in the ruins is a reminder of its often-bloody history. Weapons and armour, buckles and spurs, gaming pieces and arrowheads, Gaelic metalwork and medieval coins, all unearthed in excavations, bear witness to its importance as a location around which critical events in Irish history played out.

Mesolithic hunter-gatherers, Neolithic tomb builders, Viking raiders, Gaelic chieftains, Norman mercenaries and, today, modern sightseers, the Rock of Dunamase has been a landmark for them all.

Our heritage is not just about where we have come from, it is about our future too. This book aims to bring the Rock of Dunamase and its fascinating heritage to a wider audience and a new generation. I hope that it will entice many more visitors to Laois, to enjoy and appreciate the Rock of Dunamase, and our many other important heritage sites.

Cllr Thomasina Connell,
Cathaoirleach Laois County Council,
2022.

INTRODUCTION

The spectacular Rock of Dunamase is a natural limestone outcrop that towers over the landscape of south Laois. From its summit can be seen the Slieve Bloom mountains to the west, the flat, open land to the north and the hills to the east and south. Its shape today was moulded by the actions of nature over millennia of ancient time, creating a natural strategic fortress that was a pivot around which critical events in Irish history played out.

Today the Rock of Dunamase and its fortifications are a national monument that has been conserved by the Office of Public Works and will be protected into the future as part of Ireland's heritage.

While there is no certain record of who first built on the Rock, the grandeur of its castle ruins today stirs the imagination and makes us wonder about how people lived and used this place over thousands of years.

Left: **The Rock of Dunamase dominates the surrounding landscape.**

Chapter 1:

LANDSCAPE, GEOLOGY AND ECOLOGY

The landscape of south Laois today is dominated by steep-sided hills. Dunamase, standing 61 metres (200 feet) high and surrounded on three sides by inaccessible cliffs, is the most notable example.

The story of Dunamase can be read from its rocky core. The type and structure of its rock tell us what was happening on the earth, of changes of climate and the movements of continents and seas, when the limestone of Dunamase was slowly moulded by natural forces. The animal and plant life of ancient days can be seen in its fossils.

Its steep cliffs are the product of Tertiary weathering in the period between 65 to 1.8 million years ago. However, for the very beginnings of Dunamase we go right back to the geological period that is called the Lower Carboniferous, around 335 to 326.4 million years ago. The land of today's Laois lay beneath the waters of a shallow sea near the equator. The warm sea teemed with sea organisms like brachiopods, gastropods, corals, bivalves, sea lilies and bryozoans. When they died, their bodies were preserved as fossils in the lime-rich mud of the sea bed.

Many micro-organisms that lived in the sea, especially diatoms and radiolarians, made their skeletons or shells from silica in the water. When these creatures died, their remains sank to the bottom to form a muddy mixture known as an ooze. In the course of

Bloody cranesbill flowers in the cracks of karst limestone in The Burren, County Clare.

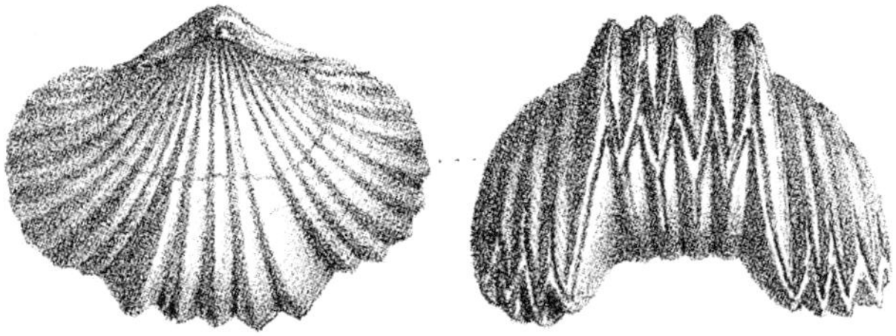

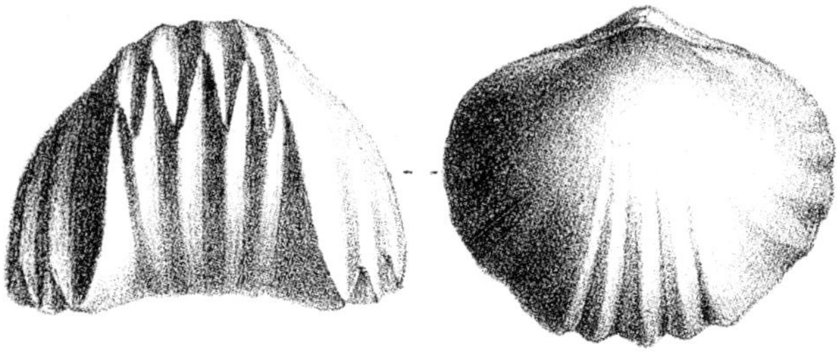

time, this began to crystallise and solidify to form very hard layers of chert, a fine-grained rock. Stone Age people later valued chert because of its hardness and they used it to make objects like tools, arrow heads and axes.

By the Tertiary Era, those underwater muds had evolved into a landscape of fissured limestone similar to today's Burren in Clare and Galway. Over time, surface water seeping underground dissolved the limestone bedrock, forming caverns and tunnels. The caverns gradually grew bigger until their limestone roofs were no longer supported and they collapsed. What was left was a series of upstanding limestone blocks called hums. The territory that became south Laois was dominated by these limestone towers rising above ground level. Dunamase is the most prominent of the surviving Tertiary-Era hums of Laois.

The climate was warmer in the Tertiary and mammals dominated life on dry land. The great reptiles, the dinosaurs, along with 80 per cent of animal species, had vanished at the end of the previous, Cretaceous, period due to changing climate, continental drift and the devastation caused when an asteroid crashed into the earth.

Much of today's Midlands was probably covered in forests of redwood, tulip tree,

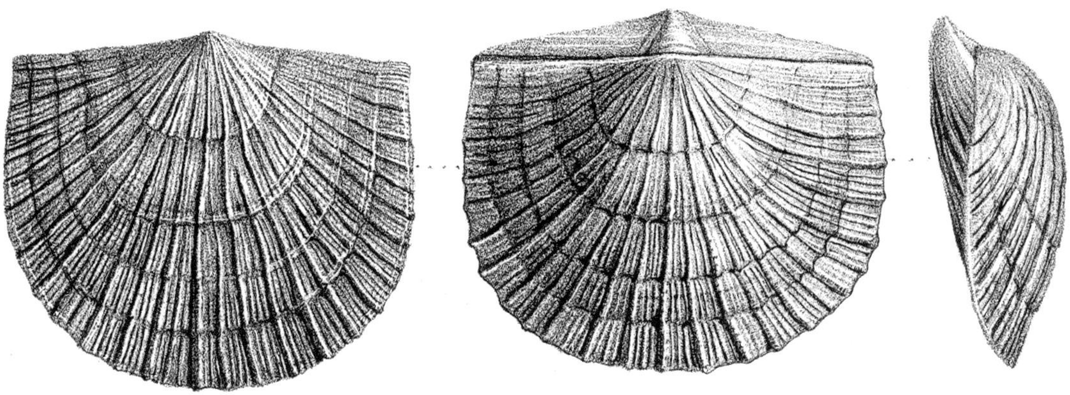

Right: **Chert axe of Danish make.**

Below: **Hums, seen here from the fortress of Dunamase, dot the south Laois landscape.**

Opposite page top line: **Fossil of Lower Carboniferous brachiopod Rhynchonella pleurodon.**

Opposite page lower line: **Brachiopod fossil Rhynchonella pugnus.**

Opposite page below: **Streptorhynchus crenistria.**

Jock Nichol 12

Japanese umbrella pine, sweetgum, sourgum and wingnut along with more familiar trees like oak, yew, maple, sweet chestnut, hazel, beech, walnut, pine, spruce, hemlock and fir. Among these forests roamed a rich variety of wildlife, ancestors of species that we associate today with tropical regions, like rhinoceroses, camels and elephants, as well as antelope, deer, horses, wild cats and dogs.

Fast forward to the start of the Ice Ages, about two million years ago. The karst landscape left by the Tertiary resembled the Burren of today but was dotted with hums. Karst is a weathered limestone bedrock, with underground drainage systems.

Over successive ice ages, glaciers, huge bodies of ice moving under their own weight, ground their way over the land of south Laois. Gradually they softened the sharp relief of the limestone towers and wore down their height. Dunamase was the first of the hums that a south-east-moving glacier met in its path and the direction of the ice sheet meant its erosive effects gave Dunamase steep cliffs on all sides except the south-east.

This happened in two processes, called plucking and crag and tail. Plucking happens when a glacier flows over bedrock and the resulting friction melts the ice. The meltwater seeps into the cracks between blocks of rock and freezes again, causing it to expand. This loosens and lifts the rock, which the glacier carries away. When there are cracks or joints in the rock, the meltwater can seep

Left: **Looking across the Tertiary landscape from the fortress of Dunamase (Original painting by Jock Nichol).**

in more easily. Plucking of its rocks accentuated the cliff sides of Dunamase. However, the southern part of the rock was sheltered from the plucking because it was in the lee of the hill, the process called crag and tail. The crag, or rock, shelters the softer material left by the glacier on the sheltered side in the form of a gradual ridge called the tail.

Because the southern side was left lower, it could be approached more easily. This meant, in later centuries, it had to be defended from attack, so the strongest walls, fortifications and ditches were built on this side. It is the side from which modern visitors come onto the Rock.

The last glacial episode dropped a blanket of glacial soil over the surviving limestone outcrops, allowing them to become covered in vegetation. Active cave formation has stopped; it is very possible that collapsed caves lie at the heart of these hills and may be discovered in time. This is what has survived from the extraordinary landscape of the Tertiary Era.

GEOLOGY

The study of the rocks of Dunamase first started about 150 years ago when the science of geology was still very young. The geologist Joseph O'Kelly, working on the first systematic Geological Survey in the mid-1850s, surveyed Dunamase. His notes were written up and published by fellow geologist George Henry Kinahan in 1859. The limestone rock of Dunamase was found by O'Kelly and Kinahan to be mostly uniform, though sometimes flaky, and full of chert bands in places. They described the limestone as being 'of a light grey or blue colour, usually massive but sometimes thin-bedded with layers and nodules of chert'.

As understanding of geology developed, however, closer inspection showed that the seemingly uniform rock structure had been laid down in a series of depositions, with over 20 distinct beds of varying texture and fossil content, which are the result of different episodes of deposition. Many of the beds contain abundant fossils, which lived in earlier eras in reef-like structures known as bioherms.

These features in the Dunamase limestone are obscured today by weathering, by vegetation growing in the soil left by glaciers and by the presence of lichen on rocks.

ECOLOGY

The cliffs and crags of Dunamase are home to a diverse range of plants and animals typical of lime-rich grassland and limestone pavement. Some of the most characteristic and abundant plants are grasses, with red fescue the most dominant grass type. Other plants include quaking grass, black knapweed, mouse-ear hawkweed, hop trefoil, white stonecrop, lady's bedstraw, wild carrot, yarrow, eyebright, wall rue, heath speedwell and the fern native to southern and western Europe, limestone polypody.

The bare limestone also supports a characteristic moss flora. Among those most likely to catch the eye are the tufted cushions of *Grimmia*, silky wefts of *Homalothecium sericeum*, and the orange tufts of goldenhead (*Breutelia chrysocoma*).

The natural grassland of the crags is a favoured habitat for snails, which make their shells from the carbonate mineral from the sedimentary rock. Species found at Dunamase include the crested vertigo snail (*Vertigo pygmaea*), the moss chrysalis snail (*Pupilla muscorum*), the ribbed grass snail (*Vallonia costata*), the blind snail (*Ceciliodes acicula*), the wrinkled snail (*Candidula intersecta*) and the heath snail (*Helicella itala*).

A round-bodied, spider-like creature with very long legs, the harvestman (*Leiobunum rotundum*), is well-adapted to the long grass. They are often better known as Daddy Longlegs. A less common species of harvestman, *Oligolophus tridens*, is found here too. This rather small species with a very long second pair of legs is most abundant in late summer and early autumn.

Grasshoppers are so plentiful they might be regarded as the emblematic species of Dunamase, occurring here in numbers rarely seen elsewhere in the Midlands. The most abundant species is the common field grasshopper (*Chorthippus brunneus*), which is recognised as easily by its song, a series of short chirps that sound like time-signal pips, as well as by sight. There are several ant species, the most noticeable being the yellow meadow ant (*Lasius flavus*), which lives in conspicuous mound-nests.

The halo of woodland around Dunamase is quite recent and few of the bushes are 100 years old. Extensive woodland is not shown

Above: **Geologist Joseph O'Kelly who studied the geology of Dunamase in the 1850s.**

Below: **Heath snail, one of many snail species found at Dunamase.**

Delicate-looking quaking grass.

From top: The spider-like harvestman or daddy longlegs; Common field grasshopper; Mound-nests of yellow meadow ants.

on the scree surrounding the Rock on the first edition of the Ordnance Survey six-inch map of 1838-41 although it does show a ring of mature trees around it, which may be those referred to by Canon John O'Hanlon.

At the end of the eighteenth century, Dunamase belonged to the Parnell family, related to the family of Charles Stewart Parnell, the campaigning politician. At that time, there was a fine grove of beech trees below the rock, which the Laois historian Canon John O'Hanlon (1821–1905) remembered seeing in his younger days. He recorded that the surrounding woods of an earlier time had been removed because they 'afforded convenient haunts for outlaws and nocturnal depredators, during the disturbed period of 1832 and 1833, when this district was under the operation of martial law'. These disturbances may have been part of the movement against the payment of tithes for the upkeep of Church of Ireland clergy.

However, when Dunamase was still a medieval fortress, there would have been no trees or bushes around it, only the scree of sharp blocks of stone that had accumulated over thousands of years following the Ice Age. These made a convenient natural *chevaux de frise*, a defensive structure against cavalry consisting of an array of spiked stones.

At the foot of the rock today, hazel coppice grows that was planted around the end of the nineteenth century. Unfortunately, an attack of gluecrust fungus (*Hymenochaete*) has killed some of them by attacking the stems then using the dying stem as a bridge to invade adjacent healthy stems.

Although the woodland floor is largely covered in ivy, there is a diverse flora of herbs that are characteristic of broadleaved woodland. Bluebell is very abundant, with woodruff, ground ivy, bugle, wood avens, wild arum, enchanter's nightshade, pignut, wood sorrel, wood violet, greater stitchwort, wild strawberry and herb Robert. The most common ferns are male fern and hart's-tongue.

Above: **Historian Rev. John Canon O'Hanlon.**

Above: Chevaux de frise at Dún Aonghasa, Inishmore, Aran Islands.

Right: Hazel trees planted in the nineteenth century.

Chapter 2:

PREHISTORY IN LAOIS

From the Rock of Dunamase little evidence of the earliest prehistoric settlers can be seen, nor has evidence of prehistoric activity been found on the rock itself. Any remains that might have been left there have probably been masked or destroyed by extensive activity on the site since the ninth century AD.

Archaeological evidence, however, tells us that this landscape has been home to people from the earliest periods of human settlement, from the movement of hunter-gatherer communities in the Mesolithic to the first farmers of the Neolithic. Bronze Age and Iron Age people buried their dead at the Great Heath, just a few kilometres away.

Some upstanding monuments survive, such as the ring-barrows of the Great Heath, standing stones and other megalithic monuments. Most of the evidence lies below ground and only comes to light through excavation as part of development projects like the M7/M8 motorways, carried out in the early 2000s. Excavations took place on Dunamase itself in the mid-1990s.

Excavations during construction of the motorways, combined with the sites and artefacts recorded by the Archaeological Survey of Ireland and the National Museum of Ireland, have added greatly to our understanding of prehistoric settlement in the region. Although relatively little evidence for Stone Age settlement has been found, very interesting evidence of settlement and activ-

ity in the Bronze Age and Iron Age has been uncovered.

MESOLITHIC

The first human settlers in Ireland are known to have lived here in the Mesolithic or Middle Stone Age, after the end of the Ice Ages but before the introduction of farming. The hunters and gatherers of the Mesolithic arrived around 8000 BC to an island that was heavily wooded, with abundant food resources in the form of fish, shellfish, game, deer, pig and edible plants like waterlily seeds. It is likely they came here by boat in small groups from along the western coast of Britain and settled along river bank, lake shore and sea coast. They fished, hunted and gathered wild fruit, berries, edible plants and nuts.

They lived a life that left little impact on the landscape. The organic tools they used have rotted away and only occasional fragments of stone tools, burnt bones, hearths, postholes or pits show they lived here. They made tools of microliths, or small flints set into a handle, and, in the later Mesolithic, larger, sometimes leaf-shaped, flints and ground stone axes.

Although no Mesolithic sites have been excavated in Laois, artefacts from this era have been found in a number of locations, providing clues about the lives of the hunter-gatherer communities. People living in the valley of the Barrow river, for example, were making and using tools made from the carboniferous limestone found in the hills of east Laois.

These people had connections much further afield. Some artefacts are made of flint that was sourced up to 200 kilometres away in Antrim. We cannot know if they were brought directly by travellers or arrived through a network of exchanges. Either way, it indicates that people were moving through the landscape of Ireland, most likely using the waterways.

Above: **Artist's drawing of setting a fish trap in the Mesolithic era.**

Opposite page: **Skirk standing stone, County Laois, is within a henge enclosure, close to a motte-type structure.**

NEOLITHIC

Around the beginning of the fourth millennium BC, people bringing a new way of life and food production arrived in Ireland. Instead of the hunting and gathering lifestyle of the Mesolithic people, the people of the Neolithic grew crops and kept domesticated animals. Growing cereals required open ground so woodland was cleared and land divided into fields. Later, open ground was used for animal grazing. They used a different set of stone tools, such as polished stone axes, made pottery and appear to have had different beliefs.

Because they were farming the land, they had less reason to move around, so they built more substantial houses and began to erect monumental megalithic tombs in which to bury their dead. Evidence suggests they lived in separate farmsteads that housed extended-family groups. Farming produced a greater, more secure, food supply that supported a higher population.

Around 3500 BC, signs appear of changes in living patterns, possibly spurred by competition for access to resources and farming land. Social organisation appears to become more complex, perhaps to manage the labour involved in larger-scale buildings and tombs.

The construction of large, elaborate passage tombs may have been intended as a display of power and a marker of territory as well as to hold the remains of the dead.

In Laois a small number of possible megalithic tombs are known, such as at Manger, Killinaparson and Knockbaun, but they are generally in too poor a condition to allow them to be identified clearly.

Finds from the bog at Clonaddoran include a wooden platform dating to the early fourth millennium BC and, among various artefacts from different periods, a stone axehead, flint arrowhead and stone spearhead. At Derryvorrigan, in the west of the county, remains of a curious, circular structure containing a central pit was found. A small amount of pottery found at the site dated it to the Early Neolithic. In the central pit was a roughly shaped, smoothed stone disc with a central perforation. This may be an early ritual site.

The Neolithic period in Ireland lasted for about 2000 years until around 2500 BC.

COPPER AGE

The working of metal spread to Ireland from the Continent in the second part of the third millennium BC, marking the end of the Neolithic. The first metal tools were made

Below: **Fire-setting as part of Early Bronze Age copper mining on Mount Gabriel, County Cork.**

Opposite page: **Stone axehead, bronze spearhead and bronze rapier found in the river Barrow at Fisherstown, Laois.**

primarily of copper and this period (2500–2200 BC) is called the Copper Age, the precursor of the Bronze Age. In Ireland up to 2200 BC, copper was sourced from a mine at Ross Island, near Killarney, County Kerry.

This period coincided with the production across Europe of a particular type of pottery, known as Beaker pottery, which in Ireland was used mainly to accompany burials. It is found, to a lesser degree, in settlement sites.

Above: **Decorated Food Vessels, a style of early Bronze Age pottery, found in a Bronze Age burial near the foot of Dunamase.**

Opposite page: **Upturned burial urn containing cremated human remains within a cist found at Strawhall, County Carlow.**

BRONZE AGE

Around 2200 BC, people learned to combine copper with tin to make bronze, marking the beginning of the Bronze Age in Ireland. More than half of the sites excavated as part of the M7/M8 motorways dated to the Bronze Age. Tin for making bronze had to be imported into Ireland from abroad, much of it from Cornwall. Early metalworkers made tools, weapons and objects of bronze and gold.

Although megalithic tombs continued in use to some degree in the Bronze Age, a range of burial practices came into use that included new forms of pottery, new monuments and, it seems likely, new rituals. In the Early Bronze Age, most bodies were buried in a crouched position, sometimes placed in a stone-lined cist or grave, and accompanied by pottery vessels and perhaps other personal items. In 1845, one such burial, accompanied by two Food Vessels, a style of early Bronze Age decorated pottery used as a grave good, was found in a circular enclosure not far from the south face of the Rock of Dunamase.

As the Bronze Age progressed, cremation became more common and cinerary urns, used to hold the ashes of the cremated dead, appeared as part of the burial rite. The burnt remains would be placed inside these large pots, which were then placed upside-down in the pit or cist. An encrusted urn burial, so named for the way the decoration was applied to the pot, was found at Shanahoe, between Abbeyleix and Mountrath.

The greatest concentration of Bronze Age burials in Laois is found in the area of the Great Heath where 14 of the county's 19 known ring-barrows have been found and where nine can still be seen. These circular enclosures consist of a ring-ditch with an external bank and sometimes a low mound in the centre. Some were excavated in advance of motorway construction in the early 2000s at the Great Heath and a little further south in Ballydavis near Portlaoise. The burials consisted of cremated bone either deposited in the ring-ditch or in a pit in the central area of the barrow.

Apart from these ring-barrows, there are relatively few Bronze Age monuments visible in the Laois landscape. There is a small number of standing stones in the county, the tallest of which is at Tullomoy, near the hill-fort at Clopook, near Stradbally. This hilltop is enclosed by a stone wall and double ditch. Excavations at other hillforts have shown evidence for Bronze Age activity but Clopook may have continued in use into the Iron Age.

At Tintore, near Rathdowney, a Bronze Age structure within an enclosure was found with a cremation and a *fulacht fiaidh* nearby. Many *fulachta fiaidh* or burnt mounds were discovered along the motorway route suggesting they were a very common site type. They consist of a mound of burnt stones that had

Encrusted urn from a cremation burial found at Shanahoe, Laois.

been heated on a fire before being put into water to heat it and, often, a water trough dug into the ground. Most of these date to the Bronze Age and are found beside a water source or in an area with a high water table. Although there are theories about their possible use as sweat lodges or for brewing beer, the discovery of animal bone suggests that they were used for cooking. The oak used to line the trough of a *fulacht* at Clonaddoran bog that contained lots of cattle bones was dated, using tree ring dating (dendrochronology), to the Late Bronze Age.

A cluster of four sites was found at Cuffsborough, near Rathdowney, including an unusual structure consisting of a circular palisade with a large central post, which may have had a ritual function.

At Cashel Bog, south of Portlaoise, another kind of ritual deposit was discovered during the milling of peat in 2011. This was the body of a young man who had been ritually murdered and his body placed either on the surface of the bog or perhaps in a shallow pool, with two hazel rods apparently either holding his head in place or marking the deposition site. His body was lying on the right side with the legs tightly flexed and the head facing to the south. The injuries found on his body included a long cut to the lower back and a broken arm.

The remains of 'Cashel Man', as he has become known, is the oldest fleshed bog body found in Europe. Radiocarbon dates tell us that he died in the Early Bronze Age, around 2000 BC. The manner of his death and deposition on a territorial boundary overlooked by Crosy Duff Hill, a possible inauguration site of the early kings of *Laígis*, suggests that this is an early example of a ritual associated with kingship and sovereignty. It is seen more often in the Early Iron Age and the occurrence of the same form of ritual killing of a young man in the Bronze Age brings the practice back from the Iron Age by at least 1500 years.

Below: **Artist's reconstruction of a Bronze Age ring-ditch burial at The Heath.**

A number of other finds have been made in the vicinity of Cashel bog. These include flat copper axes found at Colt and Crubeen, which are similar to those that would have caused the wounds in Cashel Man's back. They are now in the National Museum of Ireland.

The deliberate deposition of hoards or collections of artefacts became more common in the Bronze Age. The placing of weapons, tools or jewellery made of bronze, gold, amber and occasionally jet in a hoard could have been a ritual or votive act, or done for safekeeping, storage or simply a loss or discarding.

Above: **Tintore Bronze Age enclosure near Rathdowney, Laois.**

Opposite page: **Flat copper axeheads found in the vicinity of Cashel bog.**

In 1670, Ballymorris, near Portarlington, saw the earliest recorded discovery of a Bronze Age hoard in Ireland, consisting of a bar torc with recurved terminals, a penannular neck ring or armlet and two bars of gold. The discovery was made by the son of Farrell Mac Morris. Sadly, the items were stolen shortly after their discovery and were probably melted down and reused.

The largest recorded hoard from Laois was

found near the top of a sand and gravel ridge at Ballytegan, close to Portlaoise, during quarrying by the landowner in 1967. In the Later Bronze Age, someone had dug a simple pit about 30 centimetres in diameter and buried inside it a variety of bronze rings, two socketed axeheads, a disc-headed pin and three 'sunflower pins'. All of the items were made of bronze but the heads of two of the sunflower pins were covered with thin gold foil. This pin type is among the most common in northern Europe and two of these pins may have been imported from Denmark, while the third is probably of local manufacture.

The Ballytegan Late Bronze Age hoard.

Foreign contacts were important and wide ranging in this period. Another example is a pair of bronze bracelets found with a Bowl Food Vessel at Luggacurren, south of Stradbally, which may have had a Scottish background.

IRON AGE

Around the middle of the first millennium BC, the bronze weapon industry of the later Bronze Age declined and began to be replaced by a new metal and new technology – iron working. In Ireland and elsewhere, iron ore was sourced from bogs. Iron dissolved in water is acted on by dissolved oxygen or by bacteria to become a form of iron solid. Laois has produced interesting evidence of the transition to the use of iron. Bog iron was sourced at Clonaslee where, in 1871, long-handled shovels were found with iron ore deep in the bog.

On a large plateau in an area of rising ground at Derrinsallagh, near Borris-in-Ossory, 42 furnaces were found along with evidence of a circular structure that may have been a shelter for the iron workers at the site. Furnaces were also found on a low hill at Ballydavis. Some of the ring-barrows in this area dated to the Iron Age, showing continuity in tradition from the preceding Bronze Age. One of these ring-barrows, located on top of a low knoll just a mile south-west of the Great Heath and in sight of Dunamase, revealed interesting information about the Iron Age community living in the area.

Close to the centre of the largest ring-ditch at Ballydavis was a cremation burial dated to between the third and first centuries BC

Artefacts found with cremated remains believed to be of a woman in a large ring-ditch at Ballydavis.

accompanied by a small, decorated bronze box similar to one found in a chariot burial of a woman at Wetwang Slack in Yorkshire. Other items included a fibula brooch of a type associated exclusively with female burials of the period around the start of the first millennium AD and 86 glass beads. These artefacts, which may have symbolised the identity, status or wealth of the person, were not burnt so must have been added to the cremation after it was gathered from the

Above: **A sheet bronze disc from Monasterevin, County Kildare, demonstrates the highly skilled bronzeworking of the Iron Age.**

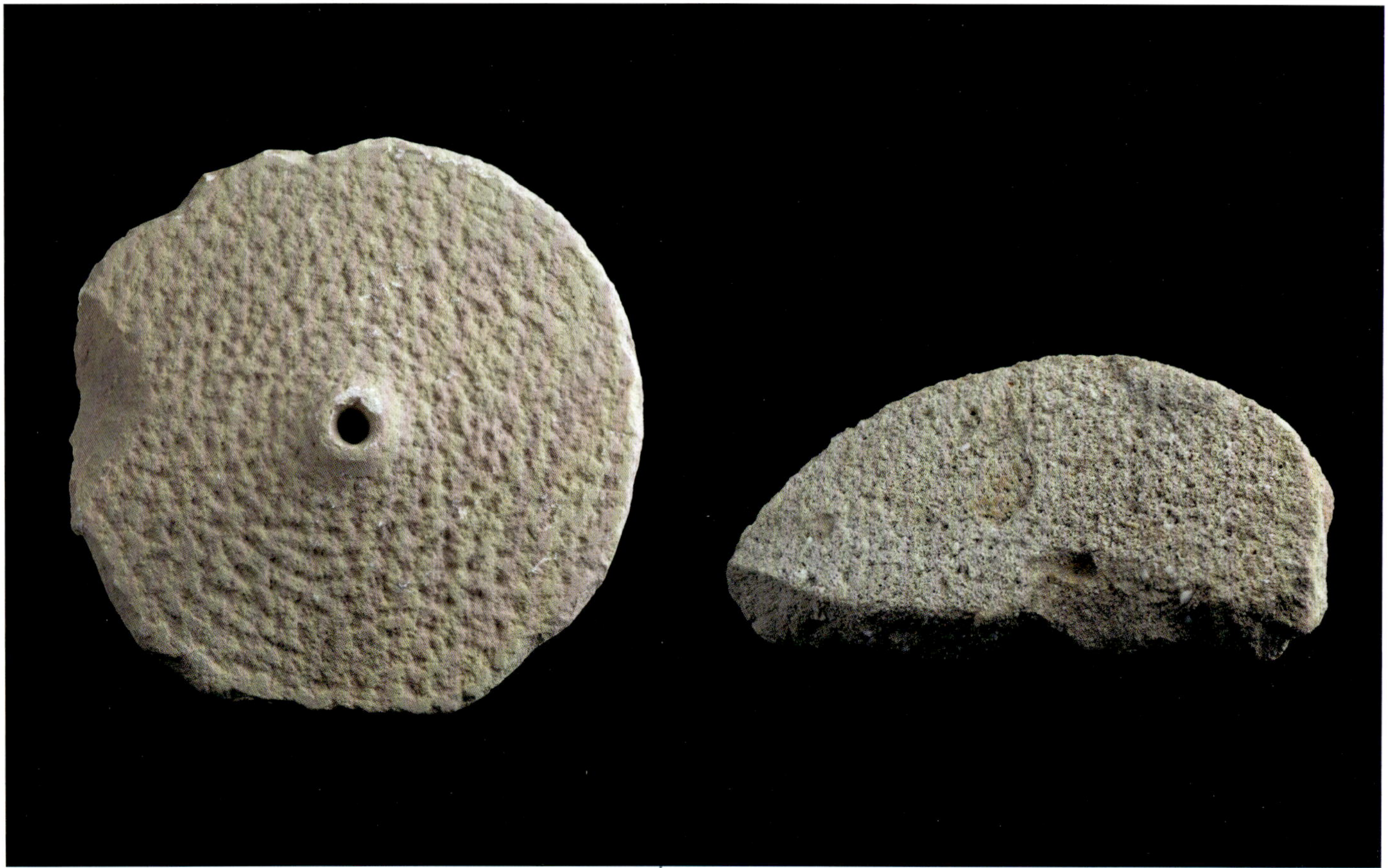

funeral pyre. Finds from the ring-ditch itself included a bronze bracelet fragment, iron nails, an iron blade, cremated bone, charcoal and fragments of iron slag. These finds indicate a high-status individual, perhaps a member of one of the families that became prominent in the area in the historical era.

Some of the artefacts found with Iron Age cremations in this area were imports, showing that the Irish were trading and interacting with the outside world. There are also indications of new groups arriving from Britain or further afield.

Many of the finds associated with the Iron Age are considered to be high status, including weapons like swords and spearheads of bronze or iron, decorated scabbards, horse equipment, brooches and glass beads and bracelets.

As well as the new iron-working technology,

Approximate dates of the prehistoric ages in Ireland	
MESOLITHIC (Middle Stone Age)	8000 – 4000 BC
NEOLITHIC (Late Stone Age)	4000 – 2500 BC
COPPER AGE	2500 – 2200 BC
BRONZE AGE	2200 – 800 BC
IRON AGE	800 BC – 400 AD

Below: **Life and death in the Iron Age; artist's reconstruction of the burial of a child at Claristown, County Meath.**

Opposite page: **Parts of an incomplete rotary quern for grinding corn.**

new bronze-working techniques were also introduced such as repoussé, a type of raised relief design on metal, which was used in the beautiful Monasterevin-type bronze discs. The type of art that decorates these items is known as La Tène and derives from the Celtic culture of the same name on the Continent; another example of the continued long-distance influences felt in Ireland into the Iron Age.

Evidence for everyday lives in the Iron Age is rarer. Pollen evidence suggests a lull in agricultural activity. However, we know that animal husbandry was important and evidence for cultivation includes another new innovation – the rotary quern for grinding grain, which replaced the less efficient saddle quern.

The area around Dunamase has been inhabited by busy, active people for thousands of years. Yet, although the Rock is such a dominant point in the landscape that it is likely to have been familiar to all of these communities, we may never know what it meant to them.

The remains of Dunamase fortress today.

Chapter 3:

HISTORY OF DUNAMASE

An Irish early medieval fortress or *dún* existed on the summit of Dunamase since at least 843 AD and probably earlier, long before the ruined Anglo-Norman fortification we see today was built. Some remains of this *dún* were found by archaeological excavations in the 1990s in the shape of two drystone walls and an earthen bank where two ninth-century metal items and an Anglo-Saxon coin of the period were found.

The area of Dunamase was located in the north-eastern corner of the kingdom of *Laígis* in early medieval times. In the sixth century, this kingdom was ruled from the royal fort of

PEOPLE AND TERRITORY

The Irish names of the early peoples of Laois and Leinster, and the territories that were called after them, have evolved over the centuries. In this guide, spelling has been standardised as follows: Dunamase is in the territory of the *Laígis*, which also is the name of their *túath* or kingdom and the name Laígis gave modern County Laois its name. The name derives from *Uí Laoighis*, the ancestral name of the *Ó Mórdha*, who rose to power in the medieval period. The *Ó Mórdha* name later evolved into the O'More, who fought against English planters in the sixteenth century.

The province and kingdom of Leinster was originally called *Laigin*, as were the people who ruled it. *Laígis* / Laois was a sub-kingdom of *Laigin* / Leinster.

The territorial unit occupied by people in early Ireland was the *túath*. These varied in size from a small area, the size of a few modern parishes ruled by a king, to larger, diocesan-sized territories. Some over-kingdoms were made up of a number of *túatha* and these, in turn, would be under the rule of a provincial kingdom.

The Irish name of Dunamase, *Dún Masc*, means the Fort of Masc.

Ráith Baccáin near the village of Rathdowney, 37km to the south-east. During most of the early medieval period, the hilltop enclosure of *Dún Ailinne*, in modern Kildare, 37km to the north-east of Dunamase, was the seat of royal power in Laigin. So Dunamase, despite its defensive advantages, was something of a political backwater in the kingdom of Leinster.

Given the lack of early written records, archaeologists look to surviving evidence of

Above: **A multivallate ringfort at Rathrar, County Roscommon.**

Opposite page: **Aerial view of Ballycarroll ringfort to the east of Dunamase with map describing it as 'Cromwell's Lines'.**

human activity to gain an insight into how and where people lived in this region in the pre-Viking period.

Ringforts, often seen in the countryside as a circular space surrounded by a low enclosing bank and outer ditch, are the remains of single-family farmsteads from the Early Medieval period. The enclosure, whose bank was often topped by a palisade, protected a circular, thatched wooden dwelling with farm outbuildings. Access was across a causeway over the outer ditch leading to a gap in the bank protected by a strong gate, usually facing east or south-east. The living area within the ringfort was typically about 30 metres in diameter. Radiocarbon dates from

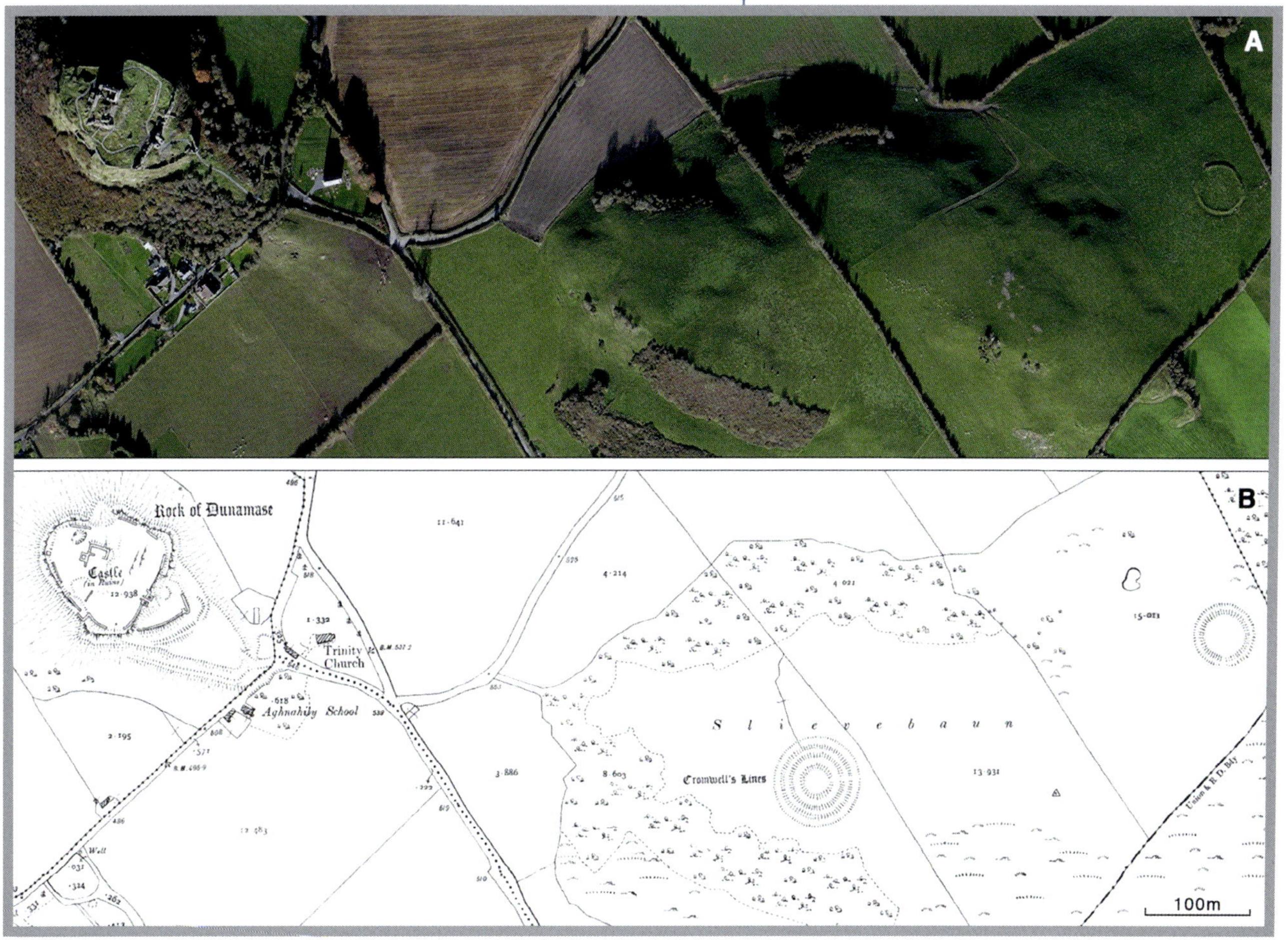

material in ringforts show they were built in large numbers after 550 AD and most fell out of use in the ninth century.

Despite the fact that the land is fertile, the lowland areas in the vicinity of Dunamase were thinly settled with ringforts. Numbers are sparse in the low-lying land to the north, which was once the territory of the *Uí Failge* people, eastward in the valley of the Barrow river and westward towards the river Nore. The early cattle farmers who built ringforts did not settle in flat but damp terrain regardless of its fertility.

Ringfort numbers increase dramatically in upland areas, however, and so the area around Dunamase itself was heavily settled, suggesting a thriving population. A large number of ringfort sites show that early dwellers took advantage of the well-drained eastern slopes of a ridge that extends from Kilmurry southwards towards Cullenagh mountain.

Among these sites the most prominent ringfort is in Ballycarroll townland, 500 metres east of Dunamase, which is sometimes named on Ordnance Survey maps as 'Cromwell's Lines'. This ringfort is trivallate, that is, it has three enclosing banks and ditches. Such trivallate ringforts are believed to have been the dwellings of the higher classes in gaelic society, perhaps the *aire forgaill* or lord. They tended to be built in a prominent position, perhaps close to a road and with a good view of the countryside. The single-bank or univallate farmstead may have been occupied by an *ocaire* or landless freeman, who rented land from the *aire forgaill*. These simpler farmsteads tended be be located close to the higher-status ringfort.

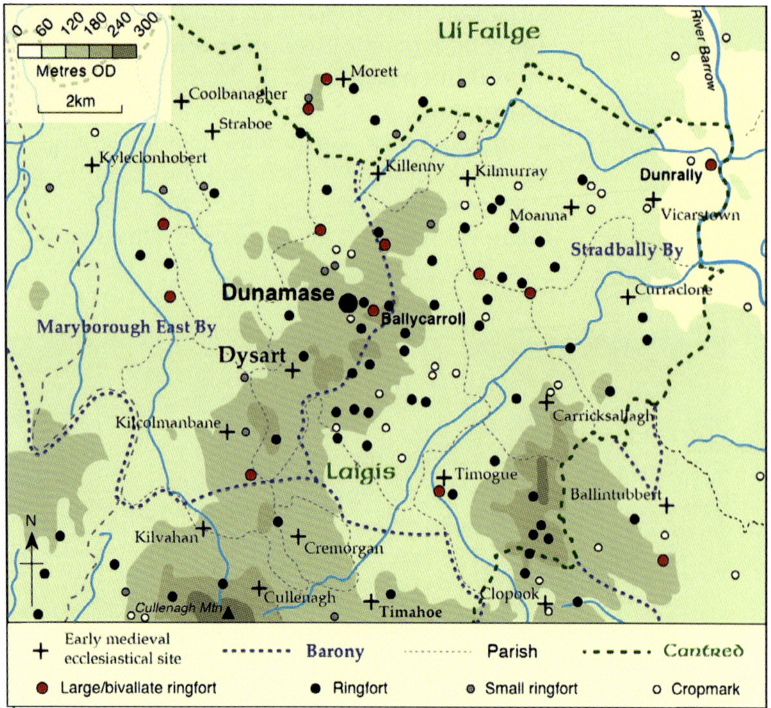

Ballycarroll's three banks displayed and defended the power and status of its owner. Such ringforts often devoted more space to their defences leaving a relatively modest living space, a mere 21 metres in diameter in the case of Ballycarroll. Gaelic nobles and lords would have rented out a lot of their farm lands to men of lower status and did not

Above: **Early medieval settlement in Laígis and the adjacent territories.**

Opposite page above: **The cross symbols indicate early medieval ecclesiastical sites located between the rivers Nore and Barrow.**

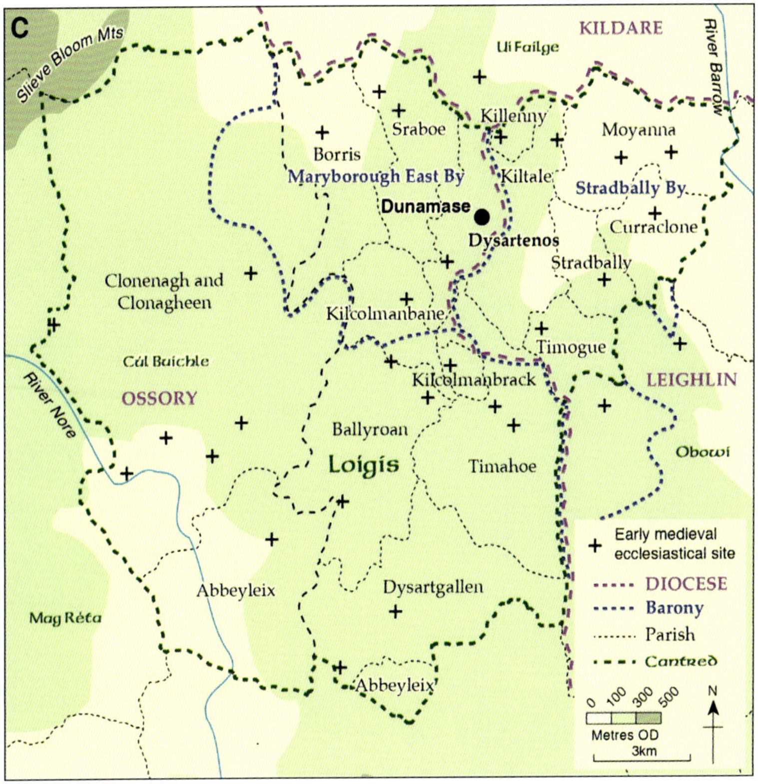

need the extra workspace required for the activities of a large farm. Like most ringforts, the entrance to Ballycarroll faces east, away from Dunamase but facing towards the single-bank ringforts on the lower hillslopes whose occupants were probably clients of Ballycarroll's *aire forgaill*. A typical univallate ringfort can be seen 300m further east of Ballycarroll.

Although there are relatively few ringforts in the area around Dunamase, ecclesiastical sites were common. There are 21 early churches in the vicinity, which put it in an 'ecclesiastical settlement' zone that includes much of *Laigin* and the eastern part of the Early Medieval province of *Mide*.

Nearest to Dunamase and in the same civil parish is *Disert Óengusa* (Dysertenos) to the south-east. The name 'disert', which means a solitary place, suggests it was an isolated hermitage when it was first established, though a monastery was later founded there. The 'Óengus' part of the name indicates a link with St Aonghas (Óengus) of Tallaght who was born in 750 AD near the nearby monastery of Clonenagh, which he entered as a youth. Seeking greater solitude, he built a cell at Disert about six miles away and became a hermit there.

Óengus later moved from Dystertenos to the monastery at Tallaght, Co Dublin, founded by St Maelruan who was part of the *Ceílí Dé* (Companions of God) spiritual movement, which practised a more austere way of life. Óengus became a prominent member of the *Ceílí Dé* and he is credited also as the author of the *Félire Óengusso* or Martyrology of *Óengus*, the Old Irish listing of early Irish saints and their feast days. He is reputed to have died in Clonenagh around 830 AD.

It has been suggested by an antiquarian source that a round tower was built at Dysertenos but if so, no traces remain. Although round towers are found at some of the most prominent post-Viking ecclesiastical sites, Dysertenos is only mentioned once in the annals, making it unlikely it was an important early foundation.

Ten kilometres south of Dunamase is Timahoe, which was one of the important early monastic sites in Ireland. Called *Tech Mo-Chua* (Mo-Chua's house), it was founded by St Crónán in the seventh century (Mo-Chua is the pet-name for Crónán). A surviving life of Mo-Chua links him also to the construction of Ireland's first stone church in Duleek, Co. Meath. The name Duleek comes from the Irish word *damhliag*, a 'stone house' as opposed to a wooden church.

The earliest dateable evidence for occupation at Dunamase is an Anglo-Saxon silver penny of Ecgberht, King of Wessex (802–39 AD), found during the 1990s excavations.

When *Dún Masc* first enters the written records the Annals of the Four Masters reports that it was raided and plundered by Vikings in 843 AD.

'Dún Masg was plundered by the foreigners, where Aedh, son of Dubdharchrich, Abbot of Tír-da-glas (Terryglass in modern Tipperary) and Cluain-eidhnach (Clonenagh near Mountrath) was taken prisoner; and they carried him into Munster, where he suffered martyrdom for the sake of God.' The prior of *Cell Dara* (Kildare, 30 kilometres to the north-east) was among the 'many others' killed that day.

The annals do not say what brought such prominent churchmen to a secular fortress in *Laígis* but the foreigners were the Vikings of Dublin. The foundation of Dublin in 841 AD had brought a significant change to their activities. Where before they had raided on a

Right: **The round tower at Timahoe with its beautiful stone doorway would have been a landmark in the landscape.**

Opposite page: **Artist's impression by James Ward (1851–1924) of a Viking fleet landing in Dublin in 841 AD.**

seasonal basis and rarely attacked the Midlands, once Dublin was established, they used it as a staging post to attack as far west as the Slieve Bloom mountains. They also had established a *longphort*, a boat camp or raiding base, on a tributary of the Barrow at Dunrally, near Vicarstown, 12km away. Dunrally means the *Dún* of Rothlaibh, who was the head of the Vikings in that region. We can speculate if, faced with this threat, an emergency meeting of prominent local church leaders and kings had been called at what might have been the new-style secular fortification at Dunamase.

The annals also hint at Viking attempts to carve out large portions of Irish territory into a Viking kingdom. In 837 AD, an armada of 120 ships had gathered on the rivers Boyne and Liffey in an attempt to conquer the kingdom of *Mide*. Further north there was a heavy Viking presence on Lough Neagh and Strangford Lough and a *longphort* at Annagassan, then called *Linn Duachaill*, where the Glyde river enters the Irish Sea in County Louth. In the south, they established a *longphort* at Woodstown on the Suir river near the town of Waterford.

The Viking encroachment represented an

existential threat to the territory of *Laígis*. From this point on, Dunamase was in the path of marauders preying on the rich pickings offered by the many monastic sites in the region. Just as it was the logical location for a major assembly, so too was it an obvious focus for a Viking assault.

The way of life represented by ringforts was coming to an end at this time and fewer, more extensive, fortifications were being constructed. *Dún Masc* may have been one of these. The Annals of the Four Masters record that in September 862 AD, Ceinnétig, king of *Laígis*, destroyed *Longphuirt Rothliabh* (Dunrally). Four years later, in alliance with the people of the adjoining territory of northern Ossory, he defeated the Vikings again. His reign, until his death in 903 AD, must have marked the greatest extent of *Laígis* power as administered from the fortress at *Dún Masc*. At this time, the Irish were gaining an upper hand over the Vikings throughout Ireland. The period between 874 AD and 912 AD was described by early medieval historians as the 'forty years rest'. The Vikings even abandoned Dublin, in 902 AD.

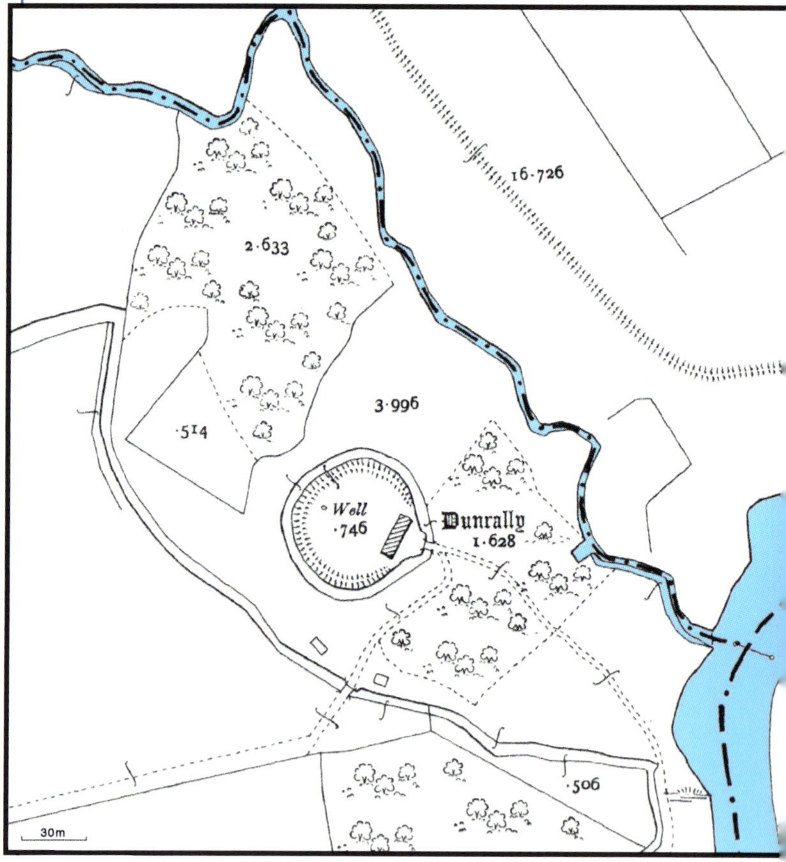

Above: **The Sea Stallion from Glendalough, replica of a Viking longboat that sailed from Dublin to Roskilde in Denmark in the eleventh century.**

Right: **Map of the site of Dunrally Viking raiding base close to the river Barrow.**

Oppopsite page: **Timahoe at the end of the eighteenth century.**

It was not to last. The Vikings returned in 913 AD and began a reign of terror that would ultimately lead to the permanent establishment of their network of coastal towns; Dublin, Wexford, Waterford, Cork and Limerick. In the reign of Ceinnétig's son and successor, Augrán, the glory days of *Dún Masc* came to an end. As part of a wider campaign by the Dublin Vikings against the Irish king of Leinster, Augaire mac Ailella, and his allies, the two sides met in battle in 917 AD at the Viking encampment at *Cenn Fuait*, just upstream from the ecclesiastical settlement of *Tech Moling* or modern St Mullins in south Carlow. Augrán, king of the Laígis, was one of the allies.

The Annals of the Four Masters record that Niall, son of Aed, king of Ireland, 'sent word to the men of Leinster that they should lay siege to the encampment from a distance. They were routed by Sitriuc grandson of Ímar in the battle of Cenn Fuait, where five hundred, or somewhat more, fell'.

Augrán of *Laígis* was among the 500 'kings, clerics and commoners' killed that day. Sitriuc went on to re-take Dublin, which was to remain a Norse stronghold until the Anglo-Norman invasion in the twelfth century. On the other hand, the kings of *Laígis* went into a decline after the defeat. Four sons and a grandson of Augrán died in rapid succession between 911 and 960. As *Laígis* power was eclipsed, much of their territory fell to the neighbouring people of *Osraige* (Ossory).

Dunamase may have been abandoned around this time and only resettled when the Anglo-Norman castle was built. No material that could be dated to the tenth and eleventh centuries was found during the archaeological excavations.

One hundred years later, when the diocesan framework of the Irish Church was established at the Synod of *Ráith Breasail* in 1111, the territory around Dunamase was divided, copper-fastening *Osraige's* expansion. Most of the kingdom (including *Dún Masc* and *Dísert Óengusa*) was assigned to Ossory. Only the far north-east, represented today by the barony of Stradbally, remained in *Laigin*.

We pick up the thread of Dunamase's story again in 1018 when the great-great grandnephew of Aughrán, Cernagh Ua Mórdha, died. Cernagh was a member of the *Ó Mórdha* (O'More) who had made the area around Dunamase one of their strongholds. Although they had risen to become the local power in the kingdom of *Laígis*, they are not recorded in the annals before this date.

From then on, the Annals of the Four Masters mention them regularly, as continually involved in internal dynastic disputes and conflict beyond the borders of their kingdom. During this period, only two Ó Mórdha kings seem to have died a natural death, in 1097 and 1149. The other kings from this dynasty were slain in 1017, 1026, 1063, 1069 (in revenge), 1091 and 1098 (by his own people). Other kings were blinded in 1041 and 1153; one was taken hostage in 1158.

THE ANGLO-NORMANS

Other forces were stirring that would bring Dunamase into a new political and military orbit and leave us the legacy of a massive fortress on the rocky stronghold.

Below: **The seal of Richard de Clare from a nineteenth-century drawing. Strongbow and Aoife's estates passed to their descendants.**

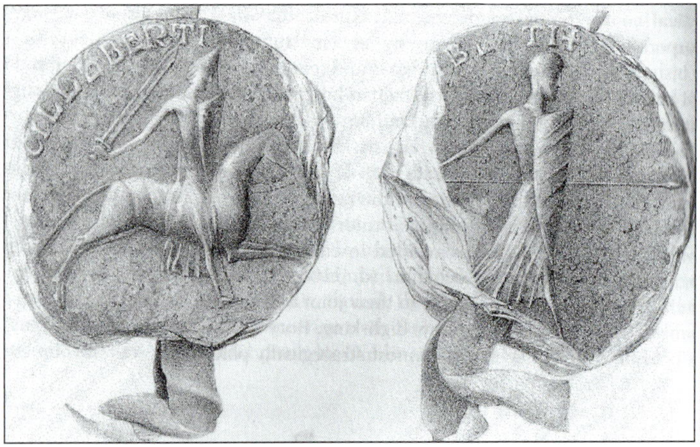

THE SYNOD OF *RÁITH BREASAIL*

The Synod *of Ráith Breasail* represented the modernisation of the Irish Church. It was concerned with creating a diocesan framework and was associated with the introduction of European modes of monasticism. Along with these major changes came the Romanesque style of architecture. The intricately carved doorway into the round tower at Timahoe is a product of the ecclesiastical dynamism within the 12th-century Irish Church despite the wider political upheavals.

In 1167, the then Gaelic king of *Laigin*, Diarmait MacMurchada (Dermot Mac Murrough), whose territory included Dunamase, had been deposed by the High King of Ireland, Ruaidrí Ua Conchobair. MacMurchada sought the help of Henry II of England in regaining his kingdom. In return for promises of land he enlisted the support of Anglo-Norman lords in Wales who mounted an invasion in 1169 and a second wave in 1170.

MacMurchada promised their leader, Richard de Clare, Earl of Pembroke (Strongbow), his daughter Aoife in marriage and the kingdom of Leinster on his death. The Norman adventurers attacked Wexford and neighbouring kingdoms and restored Diarmait to the kingship, going on to take Dublin, Waterford and in time much of the

The carved stone doorway of Timahoe round tower.

Ornate carved arch at Timahoe.

island. Strongbow married Aoife shortly after his arrival and, when MacMurchada died in 1171, he succeeded to the title of King of Leinster.

After Henry II's intervention in 1171–2, the Norman-Welsh cleric Geraldus Cambrensis (Gerald of Wales) records that Strongbow surrendered Dublin and surrounding territory along with all castles and the coastal cities to the king. He had to acknowledge also that he and his heirs held the lands he had conquered of the king and the king's heirs.

Strongbow died in 1176 and his son with Aoife, Gilbert de Clare, 3rd Earl of Pembroke, died as a minor in 1185. The inheritance, including Dunamase, then passed to their second child, a daughter, Isabel de Clare, who became Countess of Pembroke in her own right. While Isabel was a minor the estate was in royal wardship until her marriage to an Anglo-Norman nobleman, William Marshal, in 1189. Though he came from a modest background, her rank and wealth gave Marshal a prestige and power that was recognised throughout Europe. Marshal served five English kings, Henry II, Richard the Lionheart, John and Henry III and he was tutor to the Young Henry, second son of Henry II, who was crowned as junior king. He acted as a regent of England during the minority of Henry III, making him one of the most powerful men in Europe.

Isabel's right to Strongbow's estate on her marriage may have persuaded Marshal that Dunamase was his but Laois itself had been granted some years previously to another Anglo-Norman Meiler Fitzhenry, which he held direct from the King rather than from Marshal. Meiler's new territory was described as a 'hostile, difficult and wooded region' and Meiler was probably expected to subdue it. It is probable that Dunamase was held and

Above: **Portrait of King John. Dunamase was under crown control at various times.**

The marriage of Strongbow and Aoife at Christ Church cathedral, Waterford.

Left: Illustration of Richard de Clare, 2nd Earl of Pembroke (Strongbow) in Gerald de Barri's Expugnatio Hibernica.

Above: Raymond Fitzgerald Le Gros led Strongbow's advance force in the invasion of Ireland in 1170, shown in a thirteenth-century manuscript.

Opposite page: Diarmait MacMurchada, who sought Anglo-Norman support to regain the kingdom of Leinster.

Erat autem Dermitius vir
statura grandis et corpore praevalido.
vir bellicosus et audax in gente sua.
ex crebro continuoque belli cla
more voce raucisona. Timeri a
cunctis quam diligi malens. Nobi
lium oppressor. humilium erector.
infestus suis. exosus alienis. Manus
omnium contra ipsum. et ipse contra
omnes. Rothericus autem missis ad
Stephaniden nuntiis. donariis
quoque et modicis tamen promissis quam pro
missis: ut a patria in qua nullum
sibi vendicare poterat: cum pace et
amore discederet: variis suasit ver
bis. nec persuasit. Nuncii vero ad Ri
chardiden conversi ut in exteras

occupied by Fitzhenry with Marshal as his overlord and an understanding that Marshal would inherit it when Fitzhenry died. Fitzhenry tried to block Marshal from taking control of Dunamase until 1208.

In 1208 disturbances in Ireland between forces of the Crown, led by Fitzhenry, and the Marshals led by Countess Isabel, came to a head when Fitzhenry was captured and his castles and estates seized by the victor. When the dispute between the Marshals and the king was settled, Dunamase may have been transferred to William Marshal, though there is no specific statement that this occurred. Dunamase appears in the annals in 1211–12 when it was in the hands of King John, Marshal having fallen briefly out of royal favour. In 1215 an order was made to the king's officials in Ireland to hand Dunamase over to Marshal and the Marshals were in full control by 1220.

Marshal and Isabel had 10 children, five boys and five girls, but all five of their sons died without leaving an heir. On the death of their youngest son, Anselm, in 1245, the Marshal inheritance was divided among their daughters, with the Dunamase portion passing to the youngest daughter, Eve Marshal, great-granddaughter of Strongbow and Aoife, who was married to William de Braose. As Eve and William had already died, Eve's portion was split between her heirs, with Dunamase inherited by her daughter, Maud de Braose, who was married to Roger Mortimer, 1st Baron of Wigmore (1232–82).

Mortimer, from Wigmore Castle in Herefordshire, was a loyal ally of Henry III, one of the great 'marcher' lords, trusted nobles appointed by the king to guard the border lands between England and Wales. He and Lady Maud had six children. On the death of the eldest son, Ralph, their second son, Edmund, was appointed his father's heir. However, his inheritance may have been held by the crown while he was a minor.

Because William Marshal's possessions were divided among several female heirs, who were married into many of England's powerful families, the Lordship of Leinster was broken into as many as 14 parts, each of which passed into different hands. These

Above: **Roger Mortimer facing England's Queen Isabella, shown in a fifteenth-century manuscript.**

Right: **Rory Óg Ó More, leader of the Leinster Irish, shown by John Derrick in *The Image of Irelande* published in 1581.**

English noble families often had little interest in Ireland, which served to weaken the Norman hold on Irish territory.

Around 1320, Dunamase was captured by local Gaelic forces under the command of Leysagh O'More. In 1330, a different Roger Mortimer, a later descendant of the first Baron Wigmore, was executed for treason and the Mortimer lands were confiscated. The stronghold was granted to Fulke de la Freign in 1334 but he was harried by Leysagh O'More who is recorded as having destroyed Mortimer's castle. O'More died in 1342.

Although the O'Mores retook Dunamase and the surrounding territory, they did not occupy the castle and it fell into decay. Evidence from archaeological excavations suggest it was abandoned by the mid-fourteenth century, while the historical records also stop in the 1330s. There is no evidence to indicate it was occupied in the later medieval period. Yet all around the fortress, the O'Mores remained a thorn in the side of the Normon colony.

Cromwellian forces are credited in local folklore and earlier histories with the destruction of the castle but neither written records nor physical evidence have been found to confirm this.

In 1556 the Tudor monarchy began the first plantation, or planned colonisation with new English settlers, in Ireland. Under Queen Mary Tudor, the O'Mores and the O'Connors were ordered removed from their lands and their territories formed into two counties, which were named Queen's County (Laois) and King's County (Offaly). The ejected Irish fought a rearguard campaign against the plantation. The decades-long conflict between Gaelic Irish and English settlers was personified by Francis Cosby, the leader of the planters, and the O'More, the Irish chieftains.

Finally, in 1606, Cosby won the battle of Aughnahely, which was fought beside Dunamase. This led to an agreement in 1607–08 that the O'More and other Gaelic families of Laois would be transplanted to Kerry. The Earl of Thomond then took possession.

At the end of the eighteenth century, the local landowner was Sir John Parnell, Speaker of the Irish Parliament and great grandfather of Charles Stewart Parnell. He decided to restore Dunamase and create a banqueting hall at the former great hall. His changes damaged some of the original fabric of the building and gave the false impression of occupation in later medieval times.

Right: **The early structures built at Dunamase around 1200.**

Chapter 4:

HISTORY OF THE CASTLE

Dunamase today is the remains of an Anglo-Norman castle built on the site of an Early Christian Irish *dún*. It was abandoned by 1350 and slipped into decay. At some point in later centuries, it was effectively destroyed by gunpowder but we do not know exactly when or by whom.

The Rock can be divided into four parts: moving from the summit downward there is an upper ward or open space at the crown of the hill on which sits a massive stone hall, a lower ward below it, which was entered through the main gates into the castle, an inner enclosure or barbican protected by a fortified stone gateway and an outer enclosure, the lower barbican, which would have been surrounded by a wooden palisade. The inaccessible slopes of the Rock meant the summit needed few defensive structures. The emphasis lower down was on defending the main approaches from the south-east.

Archaeological excavations in the 1990s were carried out in the areas of the gate into the inner barbican, the main gatehouse with sections of the adjoining curtain wall and the hall at the summit.

The fortress was built in a series of stages starting with the ninth-century Irish *dún* and followed by three phases of Anglo-Norman construction. Archaeologists found remains of this *dún* in the form of two low, parallel drystone walls running across the eastern approach to the summit. These walls predate the rest of the masonry construction on the

Steep cliffs on all but one side protected Dunamase.

site. The outer of the two walls is free standing and sits in front of the later, Anglo-Norman, curtain wall but the inner wall is directly under the curtain wall. There was an entrance through the *dún* walls and this was reused when the gate tower that was part of the first phase of the Anglo-Norman castle was built.

Near the entrance to the *dún*, archaeologists found two pieces of decorated metalwork that were dated to the ninth century; one was a small stud found in the bank against the outer drystone wall and the other a possible horse trapping. An Anglo-Saxon silver penny of King Ecgberht of Wessex, who

Above: **The remains of an Irish *dún* ringed by protective walls; Dún Aonghasa on the Aran Islands, County Galway.**

Opposite page: **The lower slopes looking south needed defences.**

reigned from 802 AD to 839 AD, was found close to the other two pieces, giving a firm date for the *dún*, though it is probably older. The *dún* was abandoned around the tenth century as the power of *Laígis* declined. When the Anglo-Normans arrived in the late 12th century, they occupied the site and built a massive fortification.

PHASE 1 *c.*1180 AD

The earliest parts of the Anglo-Norman castle were built around 1180 AD. They comprised the large hall built on the top of the hill and a gate tower into the lower ward. At this time the upper and lower wards were probably one space. The gate tower sat directly over and re-

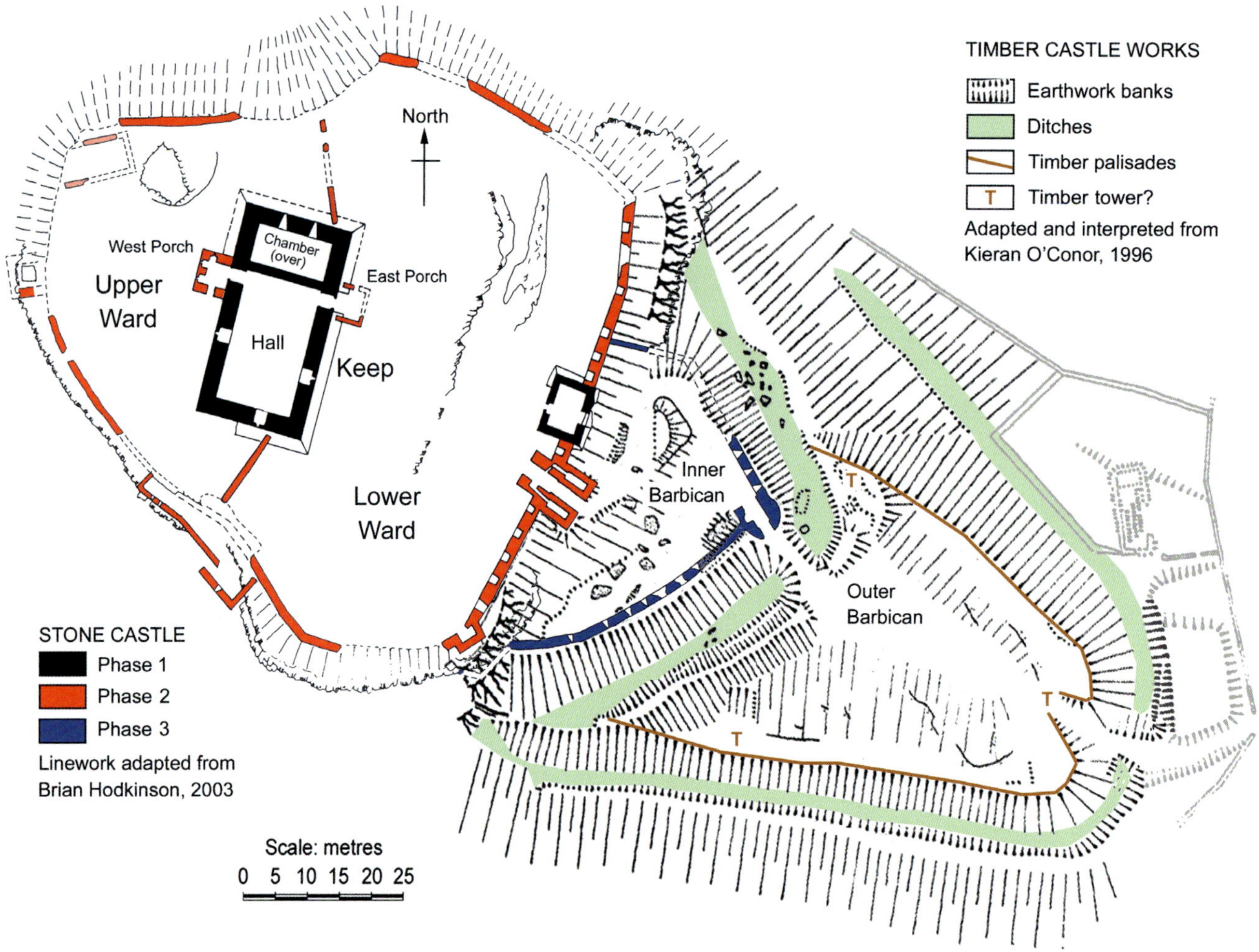

used the main entrance into the earlier *dún*. The hall and gate tower were built entirely of limestone rubble. The cut limestone that can be seen in the doorway and some windows of the hall was taken from elsewhere and added in the eighteenth century.

The gate tower was a plain, rectangular building with off-centre opposing doors. It rose to at least the height of the later curtain wall, as shown by a butt joint against this adjoining wall. The upper storey was reached via a wooden staircase and the position of one of the uprights for this was preserved in the form of a void in a batter or sloping wall

that was added later around the base of the building. A timber palisade wall ran off from either side of the gate tower, following the line of the earlier *dún* wall, and may have continued even around the crown of the hill.

The hall on the summit was a massive rectangular building, measuring 35.5m by 20m externally, with 2.8m thick walls. As with the gate tower, a sloping batter was added later around the base of the walls. The hall probably stood on open ground as there is no evidence of an early division between the upper and lower wards.

Inside the hall, a cross-wall divided the space into the main hall at the southern end and service rooms to the north. Above the service rooms there was a solar or private chamber for the lord on the first floor. This was reached by wooden stairs that rose from the main hall to a balcony running on the hall side of the dividing wall. The balcony

Above: **The entrances of the early gate tower (left) and the later gatehouse just south of it viewed from the interior.**

Opposite page: **The phases of construction on the Rock of Dunamase.**

also gave access to stone stairs above the west door that led up to the outside walkway around the roof. The hall area was single storey to roof height.

Below the balcony there would have been a screens passage running between the east and west doors around which food would have been served into the room. The west door, now partially blocked, seems to have been the formal entrance because it was wider than the east door. The hall was lit by three slit windows set in openings or embrasures in the south, east and west walls. The openings in the west and south walls probably had water cisterns inside them. No trace of a chimney has been found, so it is likely that there was a large central hearth in the middle of the hall. The smoke from the fire would have exited through louvres or slats set in the roof. The hall would have had a wooden floor suspended on joists and the roof was probably wooden too.

The two different roof directions, with the two-storey services cum solar block set crossways to the hall at its northern end make this an exceptional building among Irish castles. The roof building method is also unique in Ireland. The wall was built to a certain height, then large tie beams were laid

Above: **The hall or keep on the summit of the Rock.**

Below: **A solar in Bunratty Castle. Unlike these furnishings, the Dunamase solar would have been furnished in twelfth-century style.**

Opposite page: **Castle Rising, Norfolk, England, whose roof construction is similar to the hall roof at Dunamase.**

between the two outer long walls. On top of these was laid another beam, running the length of each wall into which the rafters of the roof were jointed. The stone wall then was built up through the skeleton of the roof to parapet level. At the solar end, there were no cross beams and the rafters were set into the beam encased within the wall. At present, the only known similar roof is at Castle Rising in Norfolk, England.

PHASE 2 *c.*1200 AD

The castle was remodelled and strengthened around 1200. A rectangular porch was added to the outside of both the doors of the hall, the old gate tower was blocked up and a new gatehouse was built just south of it. The wooden palisade was replaced in stone. Probably at this time, too, the postern gate in the lower ward was constructed in the form we see today. Cut sandstone was used for all the mouldings around arrow loops, portcullis slot, doors and windows, distinguishing it from earlier and later phases.

Defence by archery was the primary feature of the changes. The main approach to the castle is from the east. The eastern wall could be defended by archery from two levels, the wall walk and a series of 12 arrow loops set in embrasures in the wall. The new gate-

Above: **Example of a portcullis from Cahir Castle, County Tipperary.**

Below: **The original gate tower, which was blocked up (right), and the gatehouse that replaced it. The inner barbican gatehouse is in the foreground.**

Opposite page: **Detail of Bavarian stonemasons in the early sixteenth century by Rueland Frujeauf the Younger.**

house projected forward from the curtain wall line, allowing flanking fire along the curtain from ground, first floor and roof levels. A south-west tower also provided flanking fire. On all the other sides, the steepness of the hillside meant that the only defence needed was a perimeter wall.

The new gatehouse, connecting the inner barbican to the lower ward, was two storeys high. In design it consisted of a central passage flanked on either side by narrow, vaulted chambers. The absence of vaulting over the passage indicates that there was a plank floor between front and back arch, which, presumably, could have been lifted in a crisis to provide a fighting platform above and at either side of the central passage.

There was a single large room at first floor level, which was entered from the south-west corner. This room contains the only known chimney in the whole castle. This is in the north wall and it sits awkwardly in relation to the embrasure, so it is believed to be a later insertion.

The gatehouse had a number of defensive

features including a wooden portcullis possibly reinforced with iron, a wooden gate and inward-facing arrow slits. Within the gate passage the first obstacle was the portcullis. The front of the portcullis was protected by inward-facing arrow loops from the side chambers and probably by a murder hole in the room above.

The second barrier was the main gate, set just over half way up the passage and marked by an offset in the walls. It was approached along what effectively was a chasm, with fighting platforms above on either side. The inward facing loops in each of the flanking chambers were offset from one another to prevent accidentally shooting someone on one's own side.

The entrances to the chambers lay behind the gate. The entrance on the south side was wider than that on the north, presumably to give shelter for the guard or porter. Behind the main gate there were back projections inside the curtain wall, which prolonged the passage and, presumably, the fighting platform on either side. There may have been a second gate closing off the end of the passage although there is no surviving evidence for this, as neither of the back projections survive to the likely hinge level.

During this phase, the eastern opening of the old gate tower was blocked. At the same time, the inside opening was narrowed down by the insertion of stone piers against either side. Within the building, the ground was levelled upwards with a thick deposit of sandstone chips, which suggests that it may have been used as the mason's workshop during the rebuild. Subsequently, it appears to have been a smithy as the sandstone was covered with iron scale and slaggy material. No furnace has survived but this may have been in the south-west corner where there is a large hole cut from the level occupied when the smithy fell out of use. Alternatively, the sandstone may have been deliberately used to level up the ground and give a solid, fireproof floor to the smithy.

Once the castle was abandoned, the gate tower seems to have collapsed in stages rather than from a single catastrophic event. Fragments of about 10 human skulls were found in the rubble of the first phase of collapse. They had been beheaded and presumably had once been displayed on the battlements. The remains of two wicker structures were found sandwiched between layers of collapsed wall. One seemed to have replaced the other and one of them was burnt, preserving charred grain that was once stored within them. It seems that, once the castle was abandoned, this corner of the tower was used as a place for local farmers to hide their grain in times of unrest.

PHASE 3 *c.*1220–1240 AD

Between 1220 and 1240 a third phase of building took place. An inner enclosed area in front of the main wall was created by the insertion of a fortified gateway flanked on either side by a strong wall that joined the main curtain wall. This roughly triangular enclosure was entered at its apex via the D-shaped gateway and its central passage. The absence of cut sandstone found in the buildings in the earlier phase marks this as a separate development. The emphasis on defence by archery was continued, with arrow loops

Above: **Burnt circular grain store within the gate tower.**

The inner barbican gatehouse.

set in embrasures under the wall walk.

The barbican wall was continuous from below the south-east angle tower to the gateway. From the gateway north-westwards there was a short section with at least three ground-level loops, beyond which the wall is missing. The circuit was completed by a much narrower wall running at a right angle to the slope and abutting the inner curtain. This last section was little more than a screen wall but was designed to join the main curtain wall just beside a loop, to allow flanking fire along its length. Outside the wall the barbican was defended by a deep ditch or dry moat.

In its present state the gatehouse lacks its rear wall and part of its western wall and it has undergone a number of modifications that have disguised its true nature. The front of the gateway has the remains of a two-slot, counterweight drawbridge, which is not now visible above ground. The drawbridge must have opened onto a pier or trestle bridge to cross the dry moat outside. When the drawbridge had been removed from the gate, access to the inner barbican would have been very difficult. As well as a drawbridge, the arch over the gateway contained a murder hole through which stones, arrows or crossbow bolts could have been loosed on attackers.

At first floor level, there was a single chamber with three loops, one of which had access to the murder hole. The stub of the west wall preserves one side of a door giving access onto the wall walk running off south-westwards.

Probably at the time of the eighteenth century renovation the road level within the gate was lowered, pushing material into the moat to create the present pathway. Subsequent refacing within the gateway has partially obscured the scarring this caused.

Running from the carpark to the barbican gate was another enclosed area, the outer barbican, also roughly triangular in shape. It was protected by an outer ditch cut into the bedrock on two sides and by the natural slope of the hill. When surveyed in the 1990s, it was noted that there was a narrow, flattish area around the outer sides and this was taken as evidence that there had been a wooden palisade around it. This narrow base is impossible to see now because of vegetation.

Beyond the dry ditch the barbican gate would have been approached across a timber bridge connecting with the drawbridge. Below the south-west tower of the inner ward, there was a stone screen wall across the ditch between the inner and outer barbicans to stop attackers entering the dry ditch and

Above: **Bridge over a dry ditch leading to the twelfth-century gatehouse at Castle Rising, Norfolk, England.**

Opposite page: **Oliver Cromwell, painted by Peter Lely between 1653 and 1654.**

making a rush for the gate along the ditch.

The dating of this outer barbican is unclear, because there has been no excavation in this area and nothing remains of it except some earth works. The open spaces of the outer and inner barbicans and the ward areas would have had numerous wooden structures housing people and various activities that were protected by the enclosing walls.

LATER HISTORY

Both the evidence from excavations and the historical records suggest that Dunamase was abandoned finally after around 1350 and entered a period of slow decay. The historical records also stop in the 1330s and there were no archaeological finds to indicate it was occupied in the later medieval period.

There are local references to the castle having been besieged and destroyed by Cromwellian forces in the seventeenth century. Cromwell invaded Ireland on behalf of the English Parliament during the War of the Three Kingdoms, or the Irish Confederate Wars, from 1649 to 1653, and conducted a campaign of great brutality. However, no items of seventeenth-century siege warfare such as cannon or musket balls were found during excavations. Some seventeenth-century pottery was found but the amount was small and some came from the upper part of the rubble. Nor are there any references to Dunamase in seventeenth-century written sources. Local tradition does refer to a nearby ringfort, Ballycarroll, as 'Cromwell's Lines' and this is shown on Ordnance Survey maps. A nearby hill is called Hewson Hill, probably after a Cromwellian general of that name.

Undoubtedly, Dunamase is a ruin and much of the destruction was done by gunpowder. However, it is not possible to say who did this and when. It may have been put out of action in the Cromwellian period, as happened to many castles in England at the same time.

It may have been destroyed 100 years earlier during the plantation with English settlers of Leix (Queen's County) and Offaly (King's County) in the reign of Mary Tudor. A fortified camp was built to protect the settlers, the Fort of Leix, later called Maryborough, which became modern Portlaoise. The Irish led by the O'Mores fought against the settlers for many years. Dunamase,

just a few miles away, may have been seen as a base for Irish forces and a threat to the plantation that had to be put out of use.

Older histories suggest that the castle was re-occupied in the later medieval period but this is incorrect. At the end of the eighteenth century, when the local landlord, Sir John Parnell, tried to turn the hall into a banqueting hall, he brought in many late medieval

Above: **Queen Mary Tudor, who ordered the plantation of Laois and Offaly with English settlers in 1556, painted by Anthonis Mor.**

WHO BUILT DUNAMASE?

There is no record, either written or archaeological, to tell us who first built the fortifications on Dunamase or to date clearly when the three main phases of its development took place.

Possible candidates for first builder include Richard de Clare (Strongbow) or Diarmait Mac Murchada, the deposed king of Leinster, of whom it was written by Geraldus Cambrensis, 'a soldier whose heart was in the fray . . . his hand was against every man, and every man's hand against him'. Might he have reinforced the gaelic stronghold to withstand his many enemies? However, Mac Murchada's headquarters were at Ferns in Wexford. Another Gaelic ruler may even have built the first early stages of the castle.

Richard de Clare arrived in 1170, acquired the kingdom of Leinster in 1171 and died in 1176. The first construction of the Anglo-Norman castle started around 1180.

Two early Anglo-Norman adventurers are possible castle builders, Meiler Fitzhenry and Geoffrey de Costentin. De Costentin was granted Laois by Strongbow but there is no evidence he was active in the area whereas Fitzhenry, who was granted the same area at a slightly later date, was active. The conflict of interest between the two was resolved amicably by a land swap, with De Costentin securing right to land in Connacht in 1200.

Meiler Fitzhenry was one of the early Norman settlers and is recorded as having built several castles around the mid-1170s. He was granted Laois as a vassal or feudal

dependent around 1180 so he may have started the first building phase. Geraldus Cambrensis records that, when Hugh de Lacy was justiciar or king's representative in Ireland (1171–81), 'they took away from Meiler Kildare and the adjoining territory which had been given him by the Earl, and on behalf of the king gave him in exchange the province of Laois'. The description of Laois as hostile and difficult suggests that the grant was speculative and that Meiler was expected to tame his new territory.

Under this arrangement, Meiler held Laois from the king and not from William Marshal. This difference in allegiance may have been the reason for his later dispute, when he resisted Marshal taking over the castle until 1208. Since he was tenant of the castle up to 1208, he might have been responsible for the second stage of work done between 1200–1208.

Between 1200 and 1208 Meiler Fitzhenry served as justiciar and he may have been demonstrating his loyalty to John when, in 1200, he complied with the king's command to the Irish magnates for 'all persons holding lands in the marches of Ireland to fortify their castles before the ensuing feast of St John the Baptist'. Might Dunamase have been the castle he fortified for his king?

In 1208 Fitzhenry may have recognised William Marshal as his overlord but Marshal did not have physical possession of Dunamase. King John took it back in 1210 and kept it for his own use until 1215.

The third phase of building took place between 1220 and 1240. Meiler himself died in 1220 and is buried in Greatconnell priory, Co Kildare, which he founded around 1205. William Marshal died in 1219 and the Marshal family had full control of Dunamase by 1220.

Above: **Effigy of William Marshal on his tomb in Temple Church, London.**

Below: **William Marshal unseating Baldwin Guisnes in a joust, from the thirteenth-century *Historia Major of Matthew Paris*.**

cut-stone features taken from ruins elsewhere. Some of these were inserted into the building, others left to be discovered by the archaeologists. A late medieval-style door into the ground floor of the solar through the west wall has different moulding on either side and is actually part of two different doorways. Part of a stone hood mould had been left off a window on the east wall of the solar area.

Following these efforts at restyling, Parnell's son allowed the castle to revert to ruin. In 1986 it passed into state control, following which conservation works were carried out to stabilise the buildings and provide for safe public access. It is open to visitors year round.

Above: **A 1770 portrait of Sir John Parnell by the Italian artist Pompeo Girolama Batoni.**

Right: **Dunamase fortress as it would have looked around 1250.**

The inner barbican gate tower viewed from the interior

Chapter 5:

TOUR OF DUNAMASE

You can access Dunamase from the parking area beside the church at the foot of the rock. You will be following the original approach to the castle and you may notice that all the main defences were concentrated on this side.

OUTER BARBICAN

The first area you enter on the site is the outer barbican. This was a roughly triangular enclosed area at the base of the rock that was surrounded by a rock-cut ditch. Today, you cross into it by a causeway just inside the entrance to the site. Except for the pathway through it, this area is fairly overgrown but, in the thirteenth century, there would have been a wooden palisade around the edge and wooden outbuildings dotted around the inside. The barbican enclosure stretched as far as a second dry ditch in front of the stone barbican gate.

GATEWAY AND INNER BARBICAN

The path across the outer barbican leads you to the stone gateway into the inner barbican or enclosure. When you stand on the edge of the outer barbican ditch and look through the gate, you can see the road level on the interior. Try to imagine that this level continued out through the gate and onto a drawbridge. The remains of a drawbridge pit were revealed by archaeological excavation. The

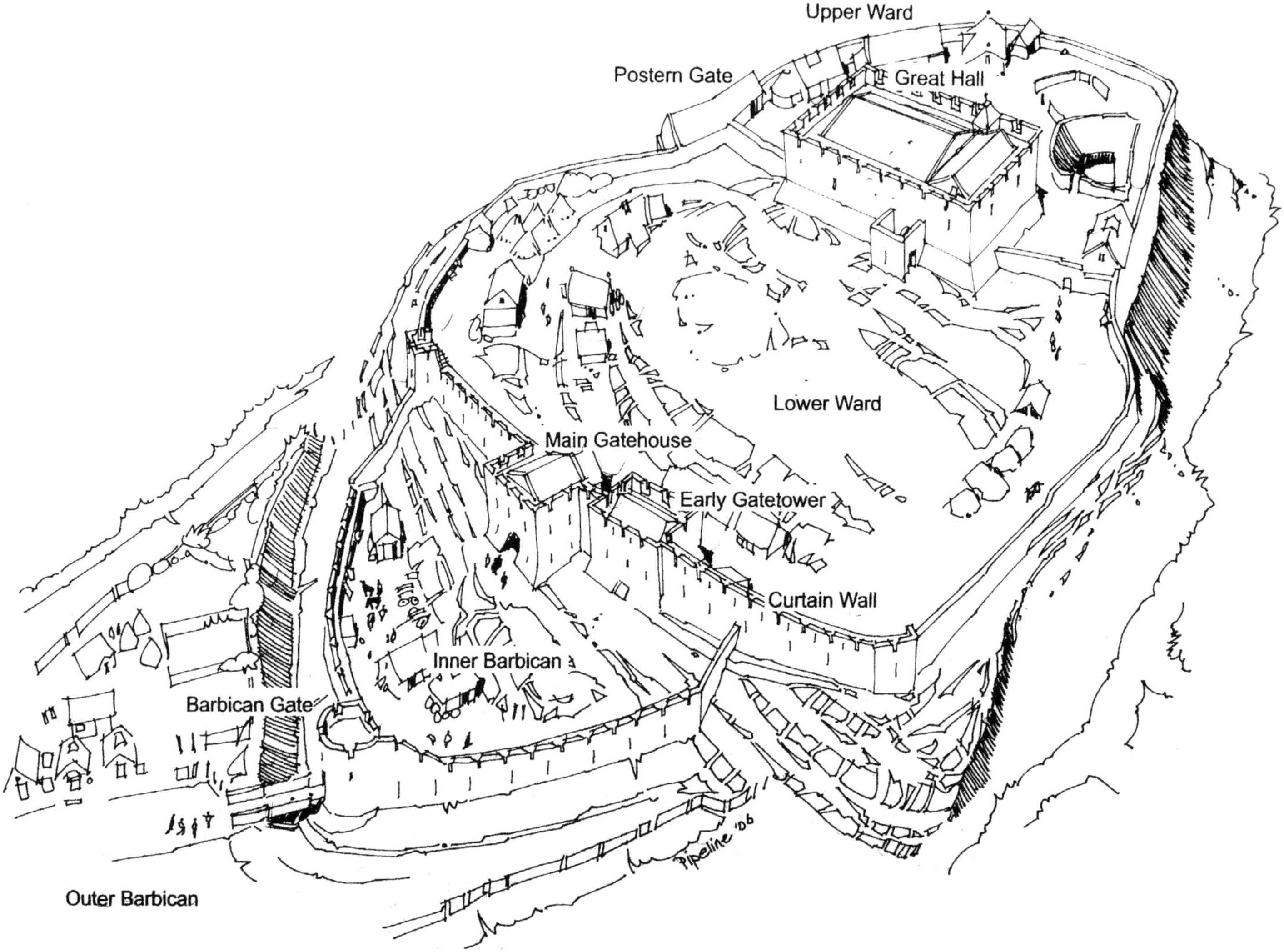

Above: **The main structures making up the fortress of Dunamase.**

Opposite page: **Remains of the gate tower leading to the inner barbican.**

drawbridge was, at most, 3.8m in length and, when down, it must have rested on a timber bridge extending into the ditch from the outer barbican.

Before going into the inner barbican, you might wish to look left along the base of the ditch to the point where it opens out to the steep drop. Looking slightly upwards to the right, one has to imagine a short length of screen wall across the moat at the far end, which would stop a rush on the drawbridge by attackers coming from the blind spot around the base of the cliff edge and running the length of the ditch to surprise the guard on the drawbridge.

As you pass in through the barbican gate tower, look up and you will see the square murder hole above in the middle of the front arch. You will see a porter's alcove on the left side of the passage. The drawbridge pit runs from the front of the tower and back about two metres. It was backfilled after archaeological excavations in 1993. The original road level through the gate was lowered and the walls either side refaced, probably in the eighteenth century.

Once through the gate, you will see the barbican walls running off to either side. On the right there is a section of standing wall with three plunging arrow loops, which is probably broken at the point of a fourth loop. Above these loops is the wall walk and steps leading upwards into the first floor of the gate tower.

MAIN GATEHOUSE AND GATE TOWER

The path rises through the inner barbican area to the main gatehouse. This is not the original entrance to the castle. To the right of the gatehouse, it is possible to see the curtain wall stopping at a vertical line. To the right of this, at the lower level, are the remains of the original gate tower. About 10 metres further to the right, there is another vertical line where the later curtain wall was built against the tower.

The gate tower is easier to understand from the inside but, before you go through the gatehouse, pause a moment outside the tower because it is built directly onto an earlier drystone wall and in front of the wall is a second low drystone wall. These drystone walls were part of the ninth-century gaelic dún. There is a clear gap in the outer wall that marks the old dún entrance and the stone tower is built over this entrance. If you

The drawbridge-pit within the barbican gatehouse, from above.

look carefully you may spot two vertical lines in the tower wall that mark either side of the blocked-up entrance.

Go back to the main gatehouse, where you will see the front is badly damaged. Enough survives to show that it was square fronted with narrow vaulted chambers at ground level on either side of a central entrance passage. The gatehouse incorporated a series

Above: **The early *dún* wall, looking northwards from the gatehouse.**

of mutually supportive defensive features. A portcullis slot can be seen at the front end of the passage. The front of this was protected by arrow loops in the chambers on either side, which are quite difficult to spot because of later destruction. However, the loops and drawbridge slot were made from sandstone, so it is possible to see the difference between this and the limestone used for most of the building.

Further up the passage, there is an arrow loop on either side. These are slightly offset

Above: **The inner gatehouse after collapse of its facade**

An internal embrasure for an arrow loop can be seen in the curtain wall on the south side of the inner gatehouse.

from each other so that an archer in one cannot fire through into the opposite chamber at his own side. About half way along the passage there is an offset or dogleg in the walls on either side, which marks

Above: **Section of curtain wall north of the gatehouse with holes for a timber hourding, a shed-like gallery that overhung the walls and allowed defenders to fire downwards.**

Right: **In the inner gatehouse, the south wall of the gate passage and the rear entry to the chamber in the south tower can be seen.**

Opposite page: **Interior view of the early gate tower with a later batter around the base in which the void for a wooden upright for a staircase can be seen (left wall angle).**

where there was a gate. Beyond the gate were the entrances into the chambers on either side; the one on the left is wider than the one on the right, suggesting that the left one was used by the guard or porter. There was probably a second gate at the very end of the passage.

The gatehouse opens into the inner ward or the main body of the castle. The main curtain wall runs away on either side to encircle the Rock. If you turn to the right you will be at the older gate tower and will be able to see its form – a plain rectangle with an off-centre passage through it. When its front gate was blocked up, the inner door was narrowed down. After this, the space seems to have been used as a mason's workshop because there was a thick layer of sandstone chips across the floor. On the surface of the sandstone there was much iron scale, suggesting that the room then had been turned into a smithy. To the right of the door as you leave, you will note a sloping wall or batter built against the base of the gate tower wall. It is not clear why this was added.

THE HALL

With the main gatehouse at your back, turn right and follow the path upwards towards the hall. You will cross the line of a wall running away from the hall to the curtain. Unlike the other side, this wall is not continuous from hall to curtain wall, indicating that the entrance to the upper ward has to have been on this side.

Following the path round the end of the hall, one comes to a door into the building. Before entering it, go around the square building on the right that sticks out from the hall. The door is on the opposite side. This building is a porch that has been added around the front of the original main door into the hall to protect it from direct attack. There is a right angle between porch door and hall door, making it difficult to ram, and there are three arrow loops within the porch. The doorway into the hall is partially blocked with later masonry, probably from the time Sir John Parnell did his restoration works in the eighteenth century.

Returning to the other door, look carefully and you will see that the two sides are not symmetrical. This is because this door was inserted later during the eighteenth-century works, when architectural fragments from other buildings were added to the hall. Before the door was punched through, the ground level on the outside was over a metre lower. If you look to the right of the door, you will see that the porch wall rises up a sloping batter set against the hall wall. This batter would have continued across the area of the later door and around the end of the hall.

Going through the door, there are chambers to the left and right within the walls. These are part of the eighteenth-century rebuilding of this corner of the hall. The door leads into the chamber end of the building and one thing you will notice is that

Above: **Original main doorway to the hall, partly blocked up during Sir John Parnell's alterations.**

Opposite page: **The new doorway was inserted in the eighteenth century, using fragments of late medieval stonework from other sites.**

the window embrasures part way up the wall show that this end of the hall had a first floor. If you look very carefully at the walls, you will begin to distinguish what is original build and what is not original. The newer work incorporates brick and the stonework uses smaller stones and is more regular.

The ground floor at this end would have contained the pantry and buttery where food and drink were assembled before being served in the hall. The kitchen would probably have been in a separate building somewhere on the top of the hill. Above the serving rooms were the private quarters of the lord.

You should now move through the dividing wall and into the main hall. The dividing wall is largely rebuilt but is on the line of the medieval one. If you stand on the inside with your back to the wall, you will see to the right the original main door of the hall. Above the door is an opening that gives access to the stairs up to the wall walk. To get to the door you would have had to go along a timber balcony, which also gave access to the lord's chamber or solar. The balcony ran along the dividing wall. One side would have been set into the dividing wall, the other set on a line of posts. The space between the posts would have been infilled to form a screen around which, at either end, the food would have been served from the buttery and pantry.

There is a smaller door into the hall directly opposite the main one. This has been blocked up but if you stand on the wall and look down, you can see that this, too, had a rectangular porch outside it and here the batter stops short on either side. From above, it is hard to see the door but if you go along the wall and down to the outside, the door is quite clear. It is worth pausing on the way to look down and take in the upper parts of the castle you have passed through.

Returning to the main hall you can see the remains of the roofing system in the form of holes for timbers on the main bit of the wall. There is a row of rectangular holes about two-thirds of the way up the wall. Above this is another row of vertical rectangular holes that are set deeper in the wall at their lower ends. What is not visible is a square hole that runs inside the thickness of the wall between the two sets. The lower holes contained tie beams that ran across the hall; onto these was jointed the internal wall beam and into this were set the sloping rafters for the roof. The wall was built up to the level of the tie beams and then the skeleton of the roof was added. Then the wall was raised through the skeleton to the wall walk, which still survives. After that, the roof proper was put on. The hall was single storey.

Within the hall there is no known fire-

Below: **How a meal in the hall might have been served. *The Peasant Wedding* painted 1566–69 by Peter Breugel the Elder.**

Opposite page: **Holes for the timber roof joists of the main hall. The gap for the original west entrance is lower right.**

Arrow loop at the junction of the curtain wall with the main gatehouse.

place, so it is assumed that it must have been central within the building with slats or a louvre set in the high ceiling to let smoke escape. It was lit by three narrow slits in embrasures, one in each of the external walls. The end of the upstanding wall on the uphill side contains half of one of the embrasures, one was more or less central in the narrow end, while the remains of one can be seen in a large collapsed section of wall on the downhill side.

REST OF UPPER WARD

Before beginning the descent, there are a few more features worth noting. Immediately outside the door you entered is a large hole. This is probably a natural sink hole in the limestone but it also may have housed the castle's water source, as there is no known well.

Following the edge of the hill in an anticlockwise direction, you come to what looks like a stone seat projecting out from the hill. This is, in fact, a latrine tower, which would have emptied down the hillside. This is the only known latrine in the castle. Looking directly out by the latrine much of what you see below lay within a medieval deer park; an alternative name for the townland of Dunamase is Park.

Carrying on in the same direction, you will come to the cross-wall from the hall to the curtain that marks the division of upper and lower ward as well as the start of the descent. To your right is the postern gate, a narrow zigzag passage to the outside. There has been little archaeological work in this area and it is not entirely clear how this area was originally laid out. Following the path down brings us to the south-west corner tower of the outer ward and along the inside of the curtain wall back to the main gatehouse. In this latter section, one can appreciate the spacing of the embrasures for arrow loops. There is an almost complete embrasure and loop in the corner where the gatehouse and curtain meet.

From the gatehouse, follow the same path back down to the parking area.

Below: **Medieval hunting park encircled by walls, from the fifteenth-century manuscript *The Master of Game*.**

ARCHAEOLOGICAL FINDS

The 1990s excavations uncovered over 5,500 registered finds that threw light on the history of the castle and its early occupants.

While organic material would have decayed over the centuries, finds of metal objects included iron weapons and armour, arrowheads, horse equipment such as spurs and buckles, locks and keys, animal bone and 10 medieval coins as well as gaelic-era stick and ring pins. There were two copper-alloy fragments of Early Christian metalwork and one tiny fragment of gold with filigree decoration that may have been part of an Early Christian object that was broken up in the thirteenth century.

Other finds included a collection of medieval pottery and some gaming pieces. Nothing suggesting domestic or female activities, such as weaving or sewing items, was found indicating the castle was mainly occupied by men. Ten skulls that had been decapitated were found in the early phases of rubble. No finds suggested that the castle had been occupied in the period after 1350 or verified local stories of a Cromwellian assault.

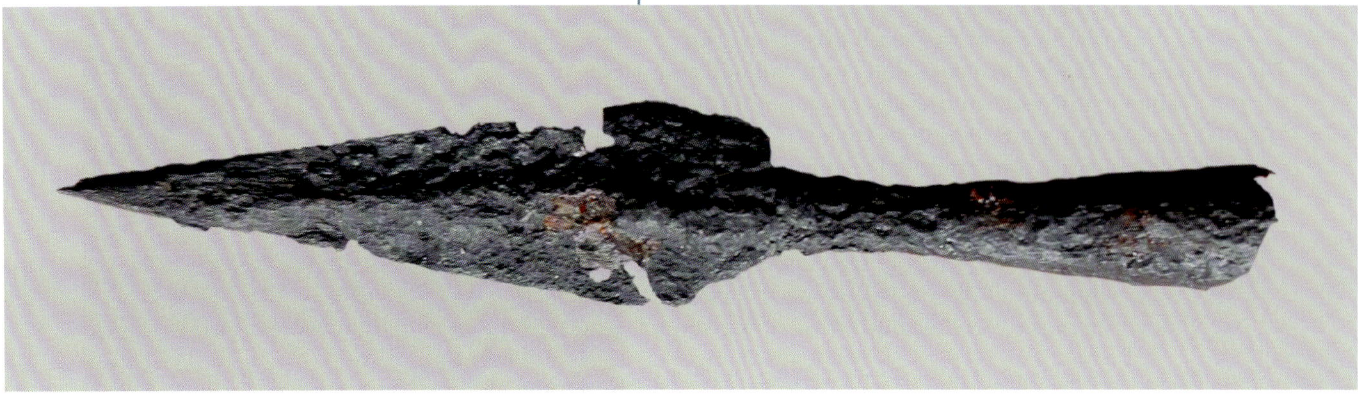

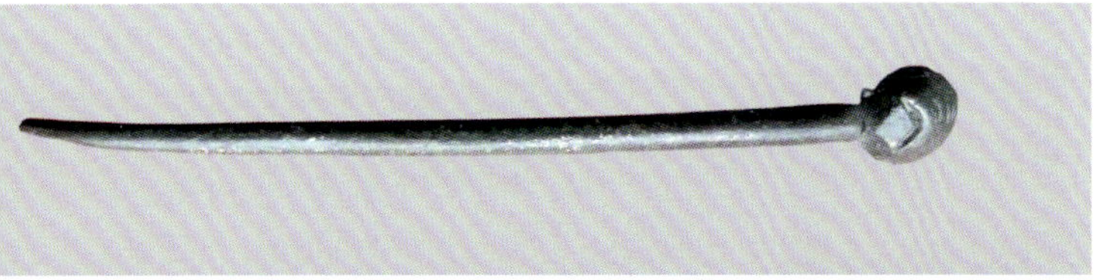

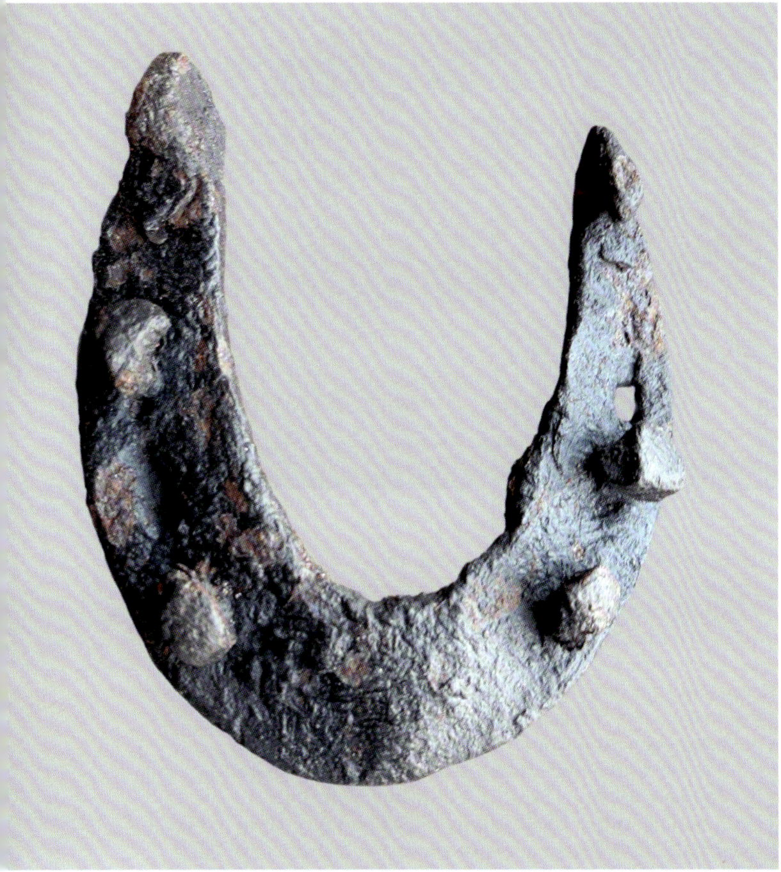

Above left: Stick pin of copper alloy, from the thirteenth century. Pins like these were usually used to fasten cloaks.

Left: Iron horseshoe dating from the thirteenth century.

Below left: Small decorated gold panel removed from a larger object, found in a thirteenth-century context but presumed to be from a 9th- or 10th-century object.

Below right: Severed heads impaled over the gate of Dublin Castle (top left) as Sir Henry Sidney marches out with his forces, from John Derrick's *The Image of Irelande*. Skulls found in the rubble at Dunamase may have been displayed like this.

Opposit page top: Thirteenth-century iron rowel spur.

Opposite page centre: Coin from ninth century found during excavations, which helped to date the remains of the earlier Irish *dún*.

Opposite page below: Socketed iron arrowhead from the thirteenth century.

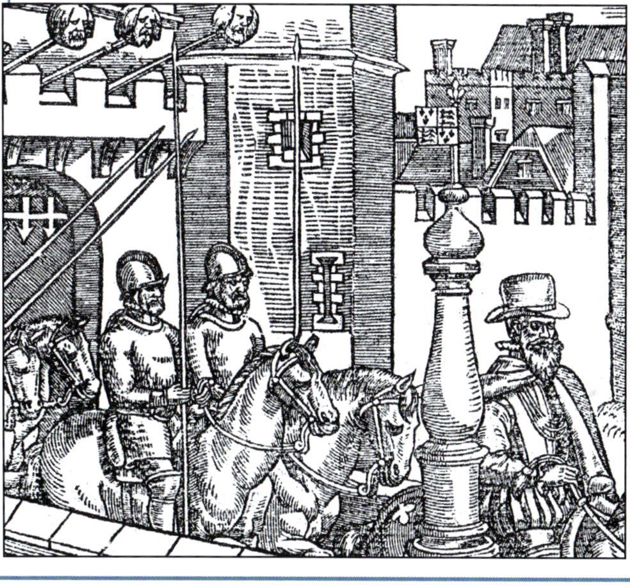

Above: The remains of the fortress today.

Opposite page: **An artist's impression of the interior of the Great Hall of Dunamase with cutaway sections showing otherwise hidden details of the construction. The hall is shown as having two pitched roofs with a gully between them. Channels cut into the stone floor in the window niche on the left (west) wall act as drains into the sub-floor space. A screens wall (cut away) divides the main hall from the chamber block where stairs rise to a first-floor balcony giving access to the main chamber or solar (right) and (ahead) to a staircase leading to the top of the wall, which is shown enclosed by a roofed timber structure called a hourd. Meiler Fitzhenry is to the left of the table at a map of the castle, planning the rebuilding of the curtain wall.**

Directions

To reach Dunamase from Dublin, take the M7 southward towards Portlaoise. Shortly before Portlaoise, where there is a sign for The Heath, leave the motorway at exit 16 and take the second left turn at the small roundabout, signposted L7830 Ballycarroll. Go along this road until you are below Dunamase. This road will bring you to the public carpark. See Google maps

CO-ORDINATES

Latitude: 53° 01′ 32.40″ North
Longitude: -7° 12′ 22.20″ West

IMAGE CREDITS

FRONT AND BACK COVERS:
Courtesy of Ken Williams.

FOREWORD:
Pages 4-5
Dunamase as it looked in 1794.
Grosse's Antiquities. Vol II, p98.

INTRODUCTION:
Pages 6-7
The Rock of Dunamase dominates the surrounding landscape.
Courtesy of Ken Williams.

CHAPTER 1:
LANDSCAPE, GEOLOGY AND ECOLOGY
Pages 8-9
Bloody cranesbill flowers in the cracks of karst limestone in The Burren, County Clare.
https://commons.wikimedia.org/wiki/File:Bloody_cranesbill_among_the_stones_-_Flickr_-_randihausken.jpg

Pages 10-11
Fossil of Lower Carboniferous brachiopod Rhynchonella pleurodon.
Courtesy of John Feehan.

Brachiopod fossil Rhynchonella pugnus.
Courtesy of John Feehan.

Brachiopod Streptorhynchus crenistria.
Courtesy of John Feehan.

Hums dot the Laois landscape.
Robert Linsdell, creative commons 2.0 https://commons.wikimedia.org/w/index.php?curid=688523106.

Pages 12-13
Looking across the Tertiary landscape from the fortress of Dunamase.
Original painting by Jock Nichol.

Pages 14-15
Geologist Joseph O'Kelly.
Courtesy of *British Geological Survey image P575775. Source: BGS GeoScenic.*

Heath snail.
Charles James Sharp. https://upload.wikimedia.org/wikipedia/commons/e/e6/Heath_snail_%28Helicella_itala%29_banded_form%2C_apical.jpg

Pages 16-17
Delicate-looking quaking grass.
www.johnshortlandwriter.com Creative Commons 2.0 https://commons.wikimedia.org/wiki/File:Quaking_Grass,_Briza_media_(8894124515).jpg

The daddy long leg or harvestman spider.
https://upload.wikimedia.org/ wikipedia/commons/c/cf/A_daddy_long_leg_aka_harvestman_spider_on_a_leaf.jpg

Common field grasshopper.
Anemoneprojectors, creative commons 2.0 https://commons.wikimedia.org/wiki/File:Field_Grasshopper_(Chorthippus_brunneus)_(8137834951).jpg

Mound-nests of yellow meadow ants.
gailhampshire Creative Commons 2.0 https://commons.wikimedia.org/wiki/File:Yellow_Meadow_Ant_mounds._Lasius_flavus._-_Flickr_-_gailhampshire.jpg

Pages 18-19
Historian Rev. John Canon O'Hanlon.
https://en.wikipedia.org/ wiki/File:John_Canon_O%27Hanlon_(Irish_writer).jpg

Chevaux de frise at Dún Aonghasa, Inishmore, Aran Islands.
Tuoermin, creative commons 3.0 https://commons.wikimedia.org/w/index.php?curid=31079529

Hazel trees planted in the nineteenth century.
Courtesy of Ken Williams.

CHAPTER 2:
PREHISTORY IN LAOIS
Pages 20-21
Skirk standing stone.
Courtesy Philip I. Powell ©.

Artist's drawing of setting a fish trap in the Mesolithic era.
Drawing J. G. O'Donoghue, courtesy of Cóilin Ó Drisceoil and TII.

Pages 22-23
Stone axehead, bronze spearhead and bronze rapier found in the river Barrow at Fisherstown, Laois.
Courtesy of National Museum of Ireland.

Early Bronze Age copper mining on Mount Gabriel, County Cork.
Courtesy of William O'Brien.

Pages 24-25
Decorated Food Vessels.
Courtesy of National Museum of Ireland.

Upturned burial urn containing cremated human remains within a cist at Strawhall, County Carlow.
Courtesy of National Museum of Ireland

Pages 26-27
Encrusted urn from a cremation burial found at Shanahoe, Laois.
Courtesy of National Museum of Ireland.

Artist's reconstruction of a Bronze Age ring-ditch burial at The Heath.
Image Dave Pollock, courtesy of Laois County Council.

Pages 28-29
Tintore Bronze Age enclosure near Rathdowney, Laois.
Courtesy of TII.

Flat copper axe head, vicinity of Cashel bog.
Courtesy of National Museum of Ireland.

Pages 30-31
Ballytegan Late Bronze Age hoard.
Courtesy of National Museum of Ireland.

Pages 32-33
Artefacts found in ring-ditch burial at Ballydavis and sheet bronze disc from Monasterevin, County Kildare.
Courtesy of National Museum of Ireland.

Pages 34-35
Parts of an incomplete rotary quern and 'life and death in the Iron Age';

artist's reconstruction of the burial of a child at Claristown, County Meath.
Drawing Dave Pollock, courtesy of Bord Gáis Éireann and Eoin Halpin.

CHAPTER 3
HISTORY OF DUNAMASE

Pages 36-37

The remains of Dunamase fortress today.
Courtesy of Ken Williams.

Pages 38-39

A multivallate ringfort at Rathrar, County Roscommon.
West Lothian Archaeological Trust (Jim Knowles, Frank Scott and John Wells), creative commons 4.0 https://commons.wikimedia.org/w/index.php?curid=51508850

Aerial view of Ballycarroll ringfort to the east of Dunamase with map describing it as 'Cromwell's Lines'.
Courtesy of Matthew Stout.

Pages 40-41

Early medieval settlement in Laígis and the adjacent territories and early medieval ecclesiastical sites located between the rivers Nore and Barrow.
Courtesy of Matthew Stout.

Pages 42-43

The round tower at Timahoe.
Courtesy of Christiaan Corlett.

Artist's impression by James Ward (1851–1924) of a Viking fleet landing in Dublin in 841 AD.
Dublin City Council, Dublin City Hall. https://commons.wikimedia.org/w/index.php?curid=36481704

Pages 44-45

The Sea Stallion from Glendalough.
Courtesy of Viking Ship Museum Denmark.

Map of the site of Dunrally Viking raiding base close to the river Barrow.
Courtesy of Matthew Stout.

Timahoe at the end of the eighteenth century.
Grosse's Antiquities Vol II p12.

Pages 46-47

The seal of Richard de Clare from a nineteenth-century drawing.
Image: *The Oxford Illustrated History of Ireland*, 1996.

The carved stone doorway of Timahoe round tower.
Courtesy of Christiaan Corlett.

Pages 48-49

Ornate carved arch at Timahoe.
Curtesy of Christiaan Corlett.

Portrait of King John.
Courtesy of Google Art Project.

Pages 50-51

The marriage of Strongbow and Aoife at Christ Church cathedral, Waterford, as depicted by painter Daniel Maclise in 1854.
Courtesy of the National Gallery of Ireland.

Pages 52-53

Richard de Clare, 2nd Earl of Pembroke in Gerald de Barri's *Expugnatio Hibernica*.
https://commons.wikimedia.org/wiki/File:Strongbow.jpg

Raymond Fitzgerald Le Gros.
https://commons.wikimedia.org/w/index.php?curid=3054712

Dermot Mac Murchada.
From Geraldus Cambrensis *Expugnatio Hibernica*, *c.* 1189.

Pages 54-55

Roger Mortimer facing England's Queen Isabella, shown in a fifteenth-century manuscript.
https://commons.wikimedia.org/wiki/File:Minature-of-Queen-Isabella-and-her-army-from-royal-ms-15-e-iv-vol-2-f316v.jpg (Copyright from the British Library)

Rory Óg Ó More, leader of the Leinster Irish.
John Derrick in *The Image of Irelande* published in 1581.

Pages 56-57

The early structures built at Dunamase around 1200.
Drawing Daniel Tietzsch-Tyler, courtesy of Laois County Council.

CHAPTER 4
HISTORY OF THE CASTLE

Pages 58-59

Steep cliffs on all but one side protected Dunamase.
Courtesy of Ken Williams.

Pages 60-61

Dún Aonghasa on the Aran Islands, County Galway.
Courtesy of National Monuments Service.

The lower slopes from the south needed defences.
Courtesy of Ken Williams.

Pages 62-63

The phases of construction on the Rock of Dunamase.
Drawing Daniel Tietzsch-Tyler, courtesy of Laois County Council.

The entrance of the early gate tower viewed from the interior.
Courtesy of Daniel Tietzsch-Tyler.

Pages 64-65

The Hall or keep on the summit of the Rock.
Courtesy of Robert Linsdell, creative commons 2.0 https://commons.wikimedia.org/w/index.php?curid=68852303

A solar in Bunratty Castle.
Courtesy of Bea y Fredi, creative commons 2.0 https://commons.wikimedia.org/w/index.php?curid=10650340

Castle Rising, Norfolk, England.
WyrdLight.com, creative commons 4.0 http://wyrdlight.com/clients.htm

Pages 66-67

The original gate tower.
Courtesy of National Monuments Service.

Example of a portcullis from Cahir Castle, County Tipperary.
Kevin King, creative commons 2.0 https://commons.wikimedia.org/wiki/File:Cahir_Castle_Portcullis_by_Kevin_King.jpg

Detail of Bavarian stonemasons in the early sixteenth century.
https://upload.wikimedia.org/wiki-

pedia/commons/c/c3/Rueland_Frueauf_d._J._003_detail.jpg

Pages 68-69

Burnt circular grain store within the gate tower and the inner barbican gatehouse.
Courtesy of Brian Hodkinson.

The inner barbican gatehouse.
Courtesy of Daniel Tietzsch-Tyler.

Pages 70-71

Bridge over a dry ditch leading to the twelfth-century gatehouse at Castle Rising, Norfolk, England.
Richard Croft, creative commons 2.

Oliver Cromwell painted by Peter Lely between 1653 and 1654.
Peter Lely (1618–1680) Oliver Cromwell (1599–1658) 1949P27. Courtesy of Birmingham Museums Trust.

Pages 72-73

Painting by Anthonis Mor of Queen Mary Tudor.
https://commons.wikimedia.org/w/index.php?curid=17617801

Effigy of William Marshal on his tomb in Temple Church, London.
Michel wal, creative commons 3.0, https://commons.wikimedia.org/w/index.php?curid=7593752

William Marshal unseating Baldwin Guisnes in a joust, from *Historia Major of Matthew Paris*.
https://www.worldhistory.org/Sir_William_Marshal/.

Pages 74-75

A portrait of Sir John Parnell, 2nd Baronet (1744–1801) by Pompeo Girolamo Batoni (1708–1787).
Painting currently held in Castle Ward, County Down. https://commons.wikimedia.org/w/index.php?curid=93276209

Dunamase fortress as it would have looked around 1250.
Drawing Daniel Tietzsch-Tyler, courtesy of Laois County Council.

CHAPTER 5
TOUR OF DUNAMASE

Pages 76-77

The inner barbican gate tower viewed from the interior.
Courtesy of Daniel Tietzsch-Tyler.

Pages 78-79

The main structures making up the fortress of Dunamase.
Drawing Dave Pollock, courtesy of Laois County Council.

Remains of the gate tower leading to the inner barbican.
Courtesy of Daniel Tietzsch-Tyler.

Pages 80-81

Drawbridge-pit within the barbican gatehouse.
Courtesy Brian Hodkinson.

The early *dún* wall, looking northwards from the gatehouse.
Courtesy Brian Hodkinson.

Pages 82-83

The inner gatehouse after collapse of its facade.
Courtesy Daniel Tietzsch-Tyler.

Internal embrasure for an arrow loop in the curtain wall.
Courtesy of Daniel Tietzsch-Tyler.

Pages 84-85

Section of curtain wall north of the gatehouse with holes for a timber hourding.
Courtesy of Daniel Tietzsch-Tyler.

In the inner gatehouse, the south wall of the gate passage and rear entry to the chamber in the south tower.
Courtesy of Daniel Tietzsch-Tyler.

Interior view of the early gate tower with a later batter around the base.
Courtesy of Daniel Tietzsch-Tyler.

Pages 86-87

Original main doorway to the hall partly blocked up during Sir John Parnell's alterations.
Courtesy of Daniel Tietzsch-Tyler.

The new doorway inserted in the eighteenth century using fragments of late medieval stonework.
Courtesy of Daniel Tietzsch-Tyler.

Pages 88-89

Holes for the timber roof joists of the main hall.
Courtesy of Daniel Tietzsch-Tyler.

***The Peasant Wedding* painted 1566–69 by Peter Breugel the Elder.**
Courtesy of Google Art Project.

Pages 90-91

Arrow loop at the junction of the curtain wall with the main gatehouse.
Courtesy Daniel Tietzsch-Tyler.

Medieval hunting park from fifteenth-century manuscript *The Master of Game*.
https://commons.wikimedia.org/wiki/File:Medieval_Hunting_Park.JPG

Pages 92-93

Archaeological finds.
Courtesy of Brian Hodkinson.

Severed heads impaled over the gate of Dublin Castle.
John Derrick's *The Image of Irelande.*

Page 94-95

The remains of the fortress today.
Courtesy of National Monuments Service.

An artist's impression of the interior of the Great Hall of Dunamase with cutaway sections to show otherwise hidden details of the construction.
Image by Daniel Tietzsch-Tyler, courtesy of Laois County Council.

BIOGRAPHIES

DR JOHN FEEHAN

Dr John Feehan has written extensively on many aspects of the natural and cultural heritage of the Irish landscape and of Laois in particular. His books include *Laois, an Environmental History* and *The Geology of Laois and Offaly*, as well as studies of Slieve Bloom and the Great Heath. He is a member of the Royal Irish Academy.

DR SHARON GREENE

Dr Sharon Greene is a research archaeologist with a particular interest in early medieval Ireland and in the archaeology of medieval walled towns. She is the editor of *Archaeology Ireland* magazine and works in community and public archaeology for Abarta Heritage. She is currently an Adjunct Research Fellow at UCD School of Archaeology (2021–2026).

DR MATTHEW STOUT

Dr Matthew Stout was a lecturer in the School of History and Geography, St Patrick's Campus, Dublin City University. His main research interests are in landscape history and early medieval Irish history. His publications include *Early Medieval Ireland 431–1169*, published by Wordwell in 2017.

BRIAN HODKINSON

Born in Southport, England, Brian Hodkinson studied archaeology at The Institute of Archaeology, now part of University College London, and Queen's University, Belfast. After college he spent many years excavating in Trondheim and other towns in Norway before moving to Ireland in the mid-1980s, where he worked on excavations first in Northern Ireland and then in the Limerick area, where he still lives. He has also worked in England, Scotland, Italy and Turkiye. In the 1990s he directed excavations at Dunamase, as well as at the Rock of Cashel and Nenagh Castle. From the late 1990s, he worked in Limerick Museum where he was later appointed museum curator. He is now retired.

PEIGÍN DOYLE

Peigín Doyle is a writer, editor and journalist who has a lifelong curiosity about the history and heritage of place and how the world might have looked through our ancestors' eyes. She has written on many aspects of archaeology and heritage.

REFERENCES

Corlett, C. 2018. An early ecclesiastical site at Timahoe, Co. Laois. *Heritage Guide* (83), *Archaeology Ireland*. Dublin: Wordwell.

Cózar, P. and Somerville, I.D. 2005. Stratigraphy of Upper Visean carbonate platform rocks in the Carlow area, southeast Ireland. *Geological Journal*. 40, pp35–64.

Crumish, R. 1992. The excavation of a fulacht fiaidh at Clonaddoran Townland, Co. Laois. *Journal of the County Kildare Archaeological Society*. pp457–472.

Delaney, D. 1996. *The Rock of Dunamase*. Vicarstown: Courtwood Books.

Desmond, S. 2007. Ancient people, hidden landscapes—the archaeology of the M7/M8 motorway scheme *IN*: O'Sullivan, J. and Stanley, M. (eds.) *New Routes to the Past*. Dublin: National Roads Authority. pp123–131.

Eogan, G. 1967. The associated finds of gold bar torcs. *Journal of the Royal Society of Antiquaries of Ireland* (97), pp29–176.

Eogan, G. 1994. *The Accomplished Art. Gold and gold-working in Britain and Ireland during the Bronze Age (c.2300-650 BC)*. Oxbow Monograph 42. Oxford.

Feehan, J. 2013. *The Geology of Laois and Offaly*. Offaly: Offaly County Council in association with Laois County Council and the Geological Survey of Ireland.

Hodkinson, B. 1995. The Rock of Dunamase. *Archaeology Ireland* (Summer) 9 (2), Dublin: Wordwell. pp18–21.

Hodkinson, B. 2003. A summary of recent work at the Rock of Dunamase, Co. Laois *IN*: Kenyon, J. and O'Conor, K. (eds) *The Medieval Castle in Ireland and Wales*. Dublin. Four Courts Press. pp32–49.

Hodkinson, B. 2003. The Sources for the History of Dunamase Castle in the Medieval Period. *Laois Historical Society Journal*. 1, pp6–20.

Holden, A.J., Gregory, S. and Crouch, D. 2006. *History of William Marshal*, 3 vols. London: Anglo-Norman Text Society.

Jukes, J.B., O'Kelly, J., Kinahan, G.H., Wynne, A. and Bailey, W.H. 1859. *Explanations to accompany Sheet 128 of the Maps of the Geological Survey of Ireland, illustrating parts of the County of Kildare and Queen's County*. Dublin: for Her Majesty's Stationery Office.

Kador, T, 2007. Ireland's prehistoric communication networks: exploring the movements of the early prehistoric inhabitants of the Barrow Valley. *Archaeology Ireland* (Summer) 21 (2), pp14–17.

Kavanagh, R. M. 1973. The encrusted urn in Ireland. *Proceedings of the Royal Irish Academy*. 73C, pp507–617.

Keeley, V. 1999. Iron Age discoveries at Ballydavis *IN*: Lane, P.G. and Nolan, W. (eds) *Laois History & Society*. Dublin: Geography Publications. pp25–34.

Kelly, E. P. and Maas, J. 1999. The Vikings and the kingdom of Laois *IN*: Lane, P. G. and Nolan, W. (eds) *Laois: history and society*. Dublin: Geography Publications. pp123–60.

Kelly, E. P. 2012. The bog body from Cashel Bog, Co. Laois. *Ossory, Laois and Leinster* 5, pp1–18.

McCotter, P. 2008. *Medieval Ireland: territorial, political and economic divisions*. Dublin: Four Courts Press.

McNeill, T.E. 1993. The Outer Gatehouse at Dunamase Castle, Co. Laois. *Medieval Archaeology*. 37, pp236–9.

McNeill, T.E. 1997. *Castles in Ireland: Feudal power in a Gaelic World*. London: Psychology Press.

National Roads Authority. 2005. Leaflet: *M7 Heath–Mayfield Motorway Scheme, Counties Kildare and Laois – Archaeological Discoveries*. https://www.tii.ie/tii-library/archaeology/Brochures%20and%20Posters/M7-Heath-Mayfield-Motorway-Scheme-Monasterevin-Bypass-Counties-Kildare-and-Laois.pdf

National Roads Authority. 2005. Leaflet: *M7 Portlaoise to Castletown/M8 Portlaoise to Cullahill Motorway Scheme, County Laois – Archaeological Discoveries*. https://www.tii.ie/tii-library/archaeology/Brochures%20and%20Posters/M7-Portlaoise-to-Castletown-M8-Portlaoise-to-Cullahill-Motorway-Scheme-Co-Laois-Updated-December-2006.pdf

O'Brien, E. 2020. *Mapping Death. Burial in Late Iron Age and Early Medieval Ireland*. Dublin: Four Courts Press.

Ó Carragáin, T. 2018. Christianizing the landscape of Mag Réta: home territory of the kings of Laígis *IN*: Lyttleton, J. and Stout, M. (eds) *Church and settlement in Ireland*. Dublin: Four Courts Press. pp60–85.

Ó Carragáin, T. 2018. Early history and settlements of the Laígis *IN*: Lane, P. G. and Nolan, W. (eds.) *Laois: history and society*. Dublin: Geography Publications. pp35–62.

O'Carroll, F. 1994. Hoards of the Later Prehistoric Period. *Archaeology Ireland* (Summer) 8 (2), Dublin: Wordwell. pp11–13.

O'Conor, K. 1996. Dunamase Castle, Co. Laois. *The Journal of Irish Archaeology*. Dublin: Wordwell. pp97–115.

O'Hanlon, Canon J. 1893. *The Poetical Works of Lageniensis*. Dublin: James Duffy.

O'Keeffe, T. 2021. *Ireland Encastellated AD 950–1550: Insular Castle-Building in its European Context*. Dublin: Four Courts Press.

Raftery, J. 1971. A Bronze Age Hoard from Ballytegan, County Laois. *Journal of the Royal Society of Antiquaries of Ireland*. 101 (1), pp85–100.

Stout, M. 2017. *Early medieval Ireland 431–1169*. Dublin: Wordwell.

Sullivan, E. 2019. The Great Heath, Portlaoise, Co. Laois. Heritage Guide (85). *Archaeology Ireland*. Wordwell: Dublin.

Sweetman, 1999. *The Medieval Castles of Ireland*. Cork: The Collins Press.